Body Control: The Pilates Way

● ●

Body Control:

● ●

The Pilates way

LYNNE ROBINSON
GORDON THOMSON

PAN BOOKS

....

ADVICE TO THE READER
Before following any advice contained in this book, it is recommended
that you consult your doctor if you suffer from any health problems or special
conditions or are in any doubt as to its suitability.

First published 1997 by Boxtree Newleaf

This edition published 1998 by Pan Books
an imprint of Macmillan Publishers Ltd
25 Eccleston Place, London, SW1W 9NF
and Basingstoke

Associated companies throughout the world

ISBN 0330 369458

9 8 7 6 5 4 3 2 1

A CIP catalogue record for this book is available from the British Library

Designed by Hammond Hammond
Illustrations by Cath Knox
Photographs by Damian Walker
Printed and bound in Great Britain
by Butler & Tanner Ltd, Frome and London

Acknowledgements

LYNNE

For their professional encouragement and advice, I will remain forever indebted to Penny and Philip Latey, Helge Fisher, Piers Chandler and, of course, Gordon.

My best teachers, however, have been my clients in Sevenoaks and London, who have trusted me to help them to help themselves. Finally, for putting up with me when I was at home, and for managing when I was not...I have to thank my daughters Rebecca and Emily.

GORDON

With thanks to all my loyal clients who have supported me consistently over the years, to my parents who have encouraged me in every career venture to date and, of course, to Lynne.

There is one unsung hero in this story – we would both like to express our gratitude and appreciation to Leigh, without whom this book would never have been written.

Finally, our thanks to our models for their time, enthusiasm and support:
Paul Fisher (Producer/Director)
Nicola Formby (Actress/model/journalist)
Paul Higgins (Futures trader)
Helen Keeble (Mother of three, now training to teach Body Control Pilates)
Dariane Pictet (Psychotherapist, with a special interest in bodywork)

Contents

Introduction   10

The Warm-up 30

Lengthening & Strengthening 56

A Sound Foundation – Foot Control 80

Flexibility & Strength 88

Working with Weights 98

The Wind-down 114

Working Out with Body Control 118

Foreword by Pat Cash

Whilst playing on the tennis circuit in 1994, I suffered a terrible injury resulting in excruciating pain in my back and down my leg. This turned out to be a herniated or bulging disk and I was told that I would need to have immediate surgery.

After the surgery, the surgeon recommended that I should either lie down or stand up for the next six weeks, no more slouching in comfortable chairs. Feeling as stiff as a post, I contacted the Australian Ballet Company on the recommendation of my trainer and my physiotherapist. Over the following weeks I commenced a very light Pilates course, two times a week. My initial reaction was amazement at how gentle, yet effective, the exercises were. I was taught how to breathe, how to improve my posture, and how to stretch and strengthen muscles I didn't even know I had while, at the same time, not risking any more damage to my vulnerable disc. I then headed to London to work with former ballerina and Pilates instructor Jenny Mills at the Royal Ballet. While I was there, I witnessed many ballet dancers with major and minor injuries come and go and, seeing their strength and flexibility, I was convinced that I would soon be fit enough to go back to full-time tennis.

Jenny was meticulous over correct body positioning and posture and, over the next two months, my stiffness disappeared, my muscles came back, my waist tightened up (I actually lost one inch off my waist) and, most importantly, my pain went.

Before I left to go back on the circuit, I started doing advanced exercises. These were some of the toughest exercises that I have ever done and I've done every fitness workout imaginable. These stretches and exercises are still in my weekly workout routine and apart from minor stiffness due to tough tennis matches, I have not had a problem with my back since. I can certainly say that without the help of the Pilates exercises, I may not be playing tennis at the top level today.

Lynne and Gordon's expertise, as outlined in this book, is the perfect way to introduce a beginner to the Pilates method and to put them on the right path to total 'Body Control'.

Foreword by Consultant Osteopath Piers Chandler D.O., M.R.O.

Does this look like just another book about exercise and 'feel-good' fitness? Well, whether you are already satisfied with your current exercise programme or you simply don't know which one to try, you will, without doubt, benefit from this book.

I know, for after trying Pilates for myself I began to encourage many of my patients to take it up, with astonishing results – this method delivers its promises.

The attraction of this book is that it is as equally suited to the great many of us who want to exercise but cannot turn up regularly for classes, as to the more athletic who may simply have pushed themselves just too far and so need Pilates for its proven rehabilitation capacities. Yet Pilates has much more to offer, because its subtle, simple methods are excellent at preventing the onset of back and postural problems, injuries and stress-related conditions.

Pilates' anatomical basis is linked to our centre of gravity and therefore our fundamental posture. Its comprehensive construction is based on eight linked principles. It is adaptable to all ages and all bodies. It emphasises Body-Mind-Emotions integrity. The latter alone justifies studying both it and the benefits it can bring.

Osteopathy is becoming increasingly recognised for its invaluable contribution to health care and general well-being, so it is refreshing to finally discover an exercise method which can genuinely complement treatment and accelerate recovery. Some patients who are referred to Pilates teachers never need any further regular treatment.

So why wait?

Introduction

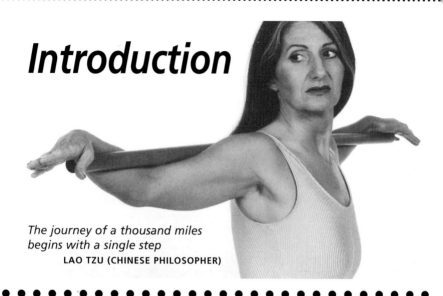

The journey of a thousand miles begins with a single step
LAO TZU (CHINESE PHILOSOPHER)

The aim of this book is to introduce you to the Body Control Method. As an introduction, we are going to start at the very beginning. As to where we end the journey ... well, that is entirely up to you. It is the journey itself that is important, and not the destination. Above all, enjoy the travelling.

Body Control is all about change. We are never too young or too old to take control of our bodies and initiate change. Our bodies are constantly changing, with the cells renewing themselves – you are not the same person today that you were yesterday; in fact, there is little of your body that is more than eight years old! We can use this to our advantage. It gives us all the chance to improve, to retrain the body and the mind, putting the balance back into both and enabling the body to heal itself.

The origins of the Body Control Method

The Body Control Method of exercise has its origins in the work of the late Joseph Pilates (pronounced Pi-lah-tis). Born in 1880 near Düsseldorf, Germany, he was a frail, sickly child who became obsessed with physical fitness to improve his body image. A keen sportsman – diving, skiing, gymnastics, boxing and wrestling were among his interests – he found himself in England at the outbreak of the First World War instructing detectives in self-defence!

Interned because of his nationality, he devised a fitness programme for his fellow internees to maintain their health and fitness levels while being held in confinement – he always claimed that his regime was the reason why not one of these internees died from the influenza epidemic that killed thousands in 1918!

After the war he returned to Germany, and it was here that he encountered the world of dance, mainly through contact with Rudolf von Laban, the originator of 'Labanotation', which is the most widely used form of dance notation. Hanya Holm included many of his exercises in her programme and, to this day, they are still part of the celebrated 'Holm Technique'. The universal appeal of his methods can be seen in how he could be attractive to the ballet companies and also a successful trainer to the Hamburg police force!

He drew the line, however, at training the new German army, which he was instructed so to do, and decided to leave for America. On the boat trip he met a nursery teacher, Clara, whom he later married – and with whom he set up his first fitness studio in New York, at an address he shared with the New York City Ballet.

It wasn't long before his studio attracted the elite of New York. Top ballet dancers came to him because his exercises perfected and complemented their traditional exercise programme. Actors and actresses, sports-people, the rich and the famous were all attracted to a workout that built strength without adding bulk, balancing that strength with flexibility, and achieving the perfect harmony between mind and muscle. The 'Pilates Method' grew rapidly in popularity but for many years remained almost exclusively the preserve of the wealthy, the famous and the beautiful! A list of its devotees proves impressive: from the world of dance: Martha Graham, George Balanchine, Suzanne Farrell, Jacques D'Amboise; screen legends Gregory Peck and Katharine Hepburn; leading current personalities such as Jessica Lange, Glenn Close, Jodie Foster, Patrick Swayze, Terence Stamp, Honor Blackman, Michael Crawford, Betty Buckley, Joan Collins, Greta Scacchi, Sigourney Weaver, Britt Ekland, Ali Macgraw and Bill Murray. Sports people include tennis star Pat Cash, women's world

champion ice-skater Kristi Yamaguchi, the Australian National Rugby Team and the Cincinnati Bengals. Madonna is a keen advocate, as is Vanessa Williams. Gordon's Body Control Studio in South Kensington is also regularly visited by many well-known faces, including Stefanie Powers, Wayne Sleep, Simon Callow, Tracy Ullman, Edna O'Brien, Olympia Dukakis, Patti Boulaye, Bonnie Langford and Sinitta. It is quite comforting to know that you are in such good company!

Fortunately the benefits of the Pilates Method meant that it would never be able to remain as exclusive. Pilates is now taught at centres throughout the world and is undergoing phenomenal growth in the United States, where there are now more than 500 studios.

Alan Herdman first brought the Pilates Method to England. Having trained with disciples of the original teaching in New York, he set up a studio with Robert Fitzgerald at 'The Place' in London, home of The London School of Contemporary Dance. It was here, 21 years ago, that Gordon Thomson trained to teach the Method. Gordon had studied dance with the Ballet Rambert and the London Contemporary Dance Theatre, and became an actor/dancer with the Scottish Opera, Glasgow Grand, English Opera Group and the Glynde-bourne Touring Company. In the mid-1970s, he sailed the Mediterranean aboard Greek luxury liners, teaching exercise based on the Pilates Method, then returning to London and dry land in 1978 to teach with the London Contemporary Dance.

In 1981, he set up his first Pilates studio at the Urdang Academy in Covent Garden, followed by one within Pineapple Dance in South

Kensington. He established his present Body Control and Rehabilitation Studio, independent of Pineapple, in 1991. Throughout the 1990s, he has been responsible for training teachers in the Pilates Method; teachers who now teach in locations as varied as Chile, New Zealand, Australia and Italy.

When Lynne Robinson approached Gordon with a request to learn from him, he was a little surprised and somewhat more apprehensive. Lynne had suffered years of back trouble, due mainly to poor posture coupled with a lack of appropriate exercise. Trained as a secondary school teacher, Lynne's focus moved to raising her two daughters, Rebecca and Emily, and to learning to travel the world as a result of her husband's career. After five years in The Netherlands, the family moved to Australia and, indeed, it was in Sydney that Lynne first encountered Pilates.

She had virtually given up hope of being free from back and neck pain and any sort of exercise – even gentle yoga – aggravated the situation. The Pilates classes she attended with Penny Latey were a turning point for, at last, she had found an exercise method that seemed to make sense. Penny and her husband Philip, a renowned osteopath, worked to put Lynne back on the road to recovery. It wasn't long before she realized that Pilates had become a major part of her life and it was then only a short step to decide to teach it.

Training with Gordon, on her return to the United Kingdom was quite an ordeal, but her body has been completely reshaped and her back problems are now a part of the history that she once taught. Once qualified, she started teaching mat-work classes in Sevenoaks, Kent and

hasn't looked back. She now works in several locations and in close relationship with local osteopaths, in particular Piers Chandler, and also gives classes at The Beadle House Clinic, a physiotherapy and sports injury centre. She has developed something of a missionary zeal in her determination to bring the benefits of Body Control Pilates to the general public.

Coming from a 'normal', non-dancing, non-sporting, background has given her an empathy with back sufferers and, indeed, with anyone new to the world of exercise. Together with Gordon, she has developed this introduction to Body Control Pilates.

No two Pilates teachers are alike and no two classes or studio sessions are the same. Joseph Pilates adapted his technique to suit the individual student, developing new mat exercises and even designing special equipment to overcome injuries and postural problems. These machines are still in use today in Pilates studios throughout the world. Everyone who came to Pilates learned something different. He did not believe in official training programmes for teachers. His early 'disciples' went on to teach their own versions of his methods. As a result, there are now many varieties of Pilates being taught. Body Control is just one of these. Instead of being a weakness, this is perhaps the Method's greatest strength. It has enabled the Method to absorb new ideas and grow, without being tied to lists of rules. Each student of Body Control Pilates will take something away from studying the Method and give something back in return.

At the end of the day, it is perhaps our own bodies that have the most to teach us!

Why is the Pilates Method so popular?

Many people reading this book will have already tried other exercise regimes. They will probably be thinking, 'What's so different about this method?' On a first glance through the book, many of the exercises will look familiar, but take a second look ... the difference between Body Control and the average keep-fit or stretch and tone session is in the way that you approach the exercises.

The Body Control Method leaves nothing to chance. It has a completely holistic approach. As with Eastern exercise programmes, it shares the training of the mind to control the body. And as your sense of body awareness and co-ordination are developed, you will be able to control every aspect of your body.

You will be concentrating on the 'core' postural muscles, learning how use those that are necessary to achieve stability in the trunk, strengthening weak muscles, lengthening those that are short and increasing joint mobility. No force is used. Slow, flowing movements are performed with control to avoid any possibility of strain.

There are no unnatural positions or boring repetitions. Each exercise is executed with your correct postural alignment taken into consideration – before you begin a movement, you must consider the angle of your pelvis and the curves of your spine. Only when you have stability in the torso and length in the spine can you think about stretching or strengthening. In this way, balance is restored to the body.

Let's take an example, such as Exercise 12, 'Spine Curls' (pages 52-3). It looks a lot like the 'Hip Lifts' you may have done in any keep-fit class but, on closer inspection, you will discover that the exercise is working on different levels. You are not just raising the hips off the ground to tone the buttocks, though that is a welcome bonus. You are, in fact, lengthening the spine, increasing the disc gaps between the vertebrae, as well as working the deepest muscles of the torso. All of this is done with the feet, knees, hips and neck in perfect alignment to correct any imbalances. The breathing helps to reinforce the benefits and the image of a wheel helps to mobilize the spine. Your awareness of your own body is heightened. You can really feel the movement taking place ... So, each exercise has been carefully designed to work on many levels. You cannot work one part of the body without referring to the rest. It's all connected so, for example, anything you do with your legs has an effect on your spine. When you move a limb, the rest of your body needs to be stable. The muscles involved in maintaining that stability and in keeping the correct postural alignment are equally as important as those used to raise the leg itself. Ignore them at your peril!

Furthermore, Body Control is not just a collection of exercises randomly thrown together, it is a complete and thorough method of physical conditioning. The exercises have all been selected to complement each other, restoring the balance of the body. Many exercise programmes fall short because they target purely 'problem areas' – or, at least, what we perceive as problem areas. In pursuit of a flat stomach, the back may be ignored. No part of the body escapes attention with this programme.

At the end of the day, however, it is the results that count. And this is where Body Control really wins the day. **Quite simply, it works ...**

The Benefits of the Body Control Method

Most people notice changes within a few weeks but everybody is different. A lot will depend on how often you practise and, of course, there are no quick fixes!

At the risk of making the Method sound like a panacea for all ills, it really can work for you on many levels. The bottom line, however, is that this book will do you absolutely no good whatsoever if you leave it on your bookshelf. Neither will it do you any good sitting on your coffee table! Use it! In six months' time it should be dog-eared through constant use – if the book is still in perfect condition then you may not be!

On the other hand, the rewards which await you can include:

■ Improved flexibility, strength, joint mobility, co-ordination, balance and alignment.

■ The elimination of bad postural habits. The body is retrained to work efficiently, so that you can move with greater economy and grace. As you hold yourself straighter, you will feel and look taller. It may even be that you grow taller, as your spine is allowed to lengthen out to its natural height.

■ Correct alignment will mean that all your vital organs will be properly supported, enabling them to function efficiently.

■ You should feel some relief from stress and stress-related disorders. Relaxation is one of the basic principles and a sense of inner calm is often felt after a Body Control session.

■ Your general health will improve. The exercises will stimulate the circulatory system, oxygenating the blood, aiding lymphatic drainage and releasing endorphins which are responsible for the 'feel-good' factor. Your immune system is given a boost so that you will have greater resistance to disease and illness.

■ You will both look and feel younger

and your skin and hair condition will improve. You may not lose weight as muscle weighs more than fat, but you will look leaner as your posture and alignment improve and everything goes back into its rightful (and original) place.

■ The Body Control Method, in conjunction with sound nutrition, can help prevent the onset of brittle bones. Recent research has shown the enormous benefits of weight-bearing exercise in the prevention (and treatment) of osteoporosis. If you are already suffering from osteoporosis, you should consult your practitioner before starting exercise. However, it is never too late or too early to start improving your bone density!

■ Relief from back pain. Body Control has a lot to offer back pain sufferers – in fact, a large proportion of our clients come to us because they have heard of the wonderful results the Method has had in the treatment of back pain. The combination of strengthening 'core' muscles within the torso, changing muscle lengths, rebalancing and relaxing the body, and teaching good postural habits makes this method highly effective in preventing back trouble.

This book is meant as a general introduction to Body Control and not as a treatment for acute back pain. However, many of the exercises within the book will be familiar to back sufferers and they may have formed part of their physiotherapy or rehabilitation programme. If you can liaise with your medical practitioner, then this book will be very helpful to you.

But is Body Control for me?

The programme given in this book is recommended for men and women of all ages who are interested in improving their total fitness, posture and appearance. However, Body Control is particularly relevant for:

✔ Sportspersons, especially those who have suffered injuries as a result of an imbalance in their muscles, notably racket sports and golf.

✔ Performers for whom good posture is vital, such as dancers, actors and musicians.

✔ Those involved in 'performance' sports – for example, dressage and skating, where postural alignment is paramount.

✔ Chronic back pain sufferers whose problems are postural-based.

✔ Sufferers of what is often referred to as Repetitive Strain Injury.

✔ Anyone wishing to return to exercise after a long break or, indeed, to take it up for the first time.

✔ The elderly wishing to maintain their independence and mobility.

✔ Women and men interested in helping to prevent the onset of osteoporosis.

✔ Any sufferers of both stress and stress-related illnesses.

✔ Anyone with a weight disorder.

As with all forms of exercise it is important to consult your medical practitioner or specialist before embarking on a new fitness regime.

Unfortunately, we have been unable to cover the specialist exercises needed for serious medical conditions. Many of the exercises given are appropriate for use by ante- and post-natal women, but it has been outside the scope of this book to provide the necessary additional information and advice to make such use safe. Hopefully, we can look forward to producing a book dedicated to the subject!

The Eight Principles

Eight basic principles underpin all the exercises.

1 Relaxation

One of the most important skills that you will need to learn while exercising, is that of how to work without undue tension. By relaxing the body before you start each exercise and by focusing your attention on the relevant area, you will find that you are able to adjust yourself into the correct position, and then hold those positions and perform the movements without over tensing. You need to use just the right amount of tension to achieve the movement. It is when you tense all the surrounding muscles, that you risk injury.

There is a difference, however, between relaxing and 'letting go' completely – the latter will result in sloppy movements and lead to a condition of collapse. The secret lies in the right combination of relaxation and concentration.

2 Concentration

'It is the mind itself which builds the body.'

Joseph Pilates was fond of quoting the German author Friedrich von Schiller. Being able to focus the mind on what each part of the body is doing all the time is quite an achievement; it will take time to master but it is well worth the effort. An exercise session which employs the mind is far more satisfying and relaxing than the session where the brain is left behind in the changing-room!

This makes a lot of sense when you consider that it is in the mind itself that all movements first originate. A movement begins, not in the muscles or the bones, but in the cerebral cortex of the brain. Usually unconsciously, we visualize a movement and then the nervous system chooses the right co-ordination of muscles necessary to carry out the task. For many tasks, this happens without our needing to think about it at all – we don't need to instruct our legs to walk, for example!

Other tasks require considerable concentration to be performed correctly eventually, they too can usually be performed without this level of awareness. If you can remember what it was like when you first sat in a car to learn how to drive, compare this to how, after practise, the movements become automatic. As you progress with the Method you will find that you will automatically 'know' what your body is doing, and where your arms and legs are. Your muscles have been re-educated. Yet you should be wary of going into automatic pilot for if you do, you will not progress. Exercises which may have seemed simple in the beginning have many levels. You will appreciate that to perform them correctly they are, in fact, quite complex .

We can use this mindfulness in another way as well. By employing images, we can help the central nervous system to choose the right combination of muscles to perform a movement. In her book *Human Movement Potential, Its Ideokinetic Facilitation*, Lulu Swiegard outlines clearly how the use of images and visualizations can lead to re-educating muscle use. As an example, if you wish to stand tall you will get better results by imagining that you are being lifted by a bunch of balloons tied to the top of your head, than if you simply say to yourself 'stand up straight'. We often use such images in Body Control to help you to achieve the right movement.

3 Co-ordination

Coupled with the need to concentrate is the need to be able to co-ordinate your movements. You must be aware of both what you are doing and also of what you are intending to do. Your 'body sense' or, to give it its proper name, your kinesthetic sense, can be greatly improved by Body Control.

Throughout your body there are sensory nerves which can register where, for example, your hands, arms and feet are and what they are actually doing. These nerves are essential to co-ordination, sending messages which can be interpreted and acted upon. The cerebellum is one of the crucial areas of the brain which control movement, co-ordination and posture. It must process information not just about where you are in space, but also where you have been and where you will be. Think about the escalator ... as your foot steps forward, your brain anticipates and allows for the movement of the stair – if it is out of order, its non-movement throws you momentarily off balance.

In order to develop your kinesthetic sense you need to listen carefully to the messages being sent back from these sensory nerves and be able to interpret them. The central nervous system can then choose the best possible combination of muscles to act. At first it is trial and error. As a movement becomes more familiar, you pass through the awkward, clumsy stage and the movement is refined. It is the process of acquiring these new skills, the training of the mind and body communication channels, which is so very important. It will stand you in good stead in everything you do, not just exercising.

In practical terms, when you begin the exercises, you will probably discover that your arms and legs have a mind of their own. You think that your foot is flexed, yet in reality it may be pointed! The exercises have been designed to increase that level of control gradually. You will regain control of your body. It will seem impossible at first for the instructions are often complex and it is hard to have to think of so many things at once – 'How can I lift my leg, anchor my back, flex my foot and stretch my neck all at the same time?' Some of us are gifted with better co-ordination than others, but happily, it is a skill that can be learned.

Body Control will soon put you right back in the driving seat.

4 Alignment

The body is a closed system – if one part of it is out of alignment, then the whole structure is altered. Imagine a building with foundations that are uneven. Its stability will obviously be affected. But so too will all the internal workings – the plumbing, the electricity, the plastering, etc. Your general health and well-being are affected by your posture. View the body as a set of building blocks ...

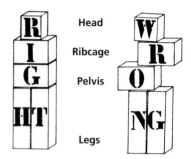

You can quite easily see the repercussions of misalignment.

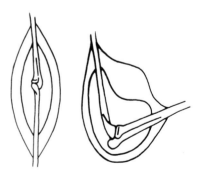

For a muscle to contract effectively, the opposing muscle must be able to lengthen and release.

Note how the three main body weights are balanced over each other.

Our centre of gravity is behind the navel, usually in front of the 3rd and 4th lumbar vertebrae.

while the opposing group need to lengthen to allow that movement.

Over-dominance by one of the muscles in a movement means that the others work less. Muscles can also become too tight or too stretched. Either way, the system is upset and it then becomes only a matter of time before pain will set in.

The good news is that bad alignment can be corrected with a conditioning programme. Body Control is all about rebalancing the body, and that is precisely why we are so pedantic about the placement of the feet, neck and limbs. You are aiming to realign the body.

If you follow the exercises regularly, it will not be long before you or your friends will notice that there is an improvement in your bodyline – and remember that the external changes are accompanied by internal changes too. Your vital organs will be properly supported in their intended positions by firm muscles, enabling them to function much more efficiently.

There is an ideal to which we can aspire (see left).

Notice the alignment of the spine and the pelvis. If you like, you can compare it with those on pages 124–5. A neutral position, with the back neither too arched nor too flat, is the goal.

Whether we are sitting, lying or standing, the relationship between the pelvis and the spine is very important.

You can try the following simple experiment to find the correct placement:

Your body has been designed so that its weight is transferred through the centre of each joint – the weight of the head through the first vertebra, the weight of the head and first vertebra through the centre of the second vertebra and so forth through the spine, the centre of the hip, the knee, the ankle and the foot. If (through injury, poor posture or sloppy exercise), the weight is displaced toward the back, front or side, this then puts a strain on the joints, the bones, the ligaments and so on. Muscles work in groups, never alone, to move bones. They can only pull, they never push. One group will contract to produce a movement,

Lie on your back with your knees bent, neck long, feet long, elbows open and your hands resting on your abdomen. Imagine that there is a compass resting on top of your abdomen.

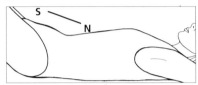

Tilt your pelvis, using the abdominal muscles, so that the focal point is on 'North'. The waist is flattened, the curve lost.

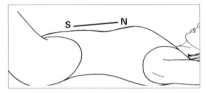

Now tilt your pelvis so that it is pointing to the 'South'. The low back is over-arched.

Repeat several times, and then find the neutral position between North and South, the pelvis being tilted neither way but balanced in the middle. The same applies to West and East – tilt the pelvis in each direction, and then find that neutral position. The natural curves are maintained.

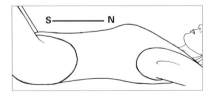

Remember this neutral positioning and remember the 'North to South' balance – we will be reminding you of it throughout the book.

5 Breathing

It is a sad fact that very few of us breathe properly. Nature gave us a wonderful pair of lungs (as parents of new-born babies will testify). We use only a fraction of their full capacity and, as a result, deny ourselves the benefits that accompany correct breathing.

It is vital to learn how to breathe fully to get the blood pumping, thereby enabling it to stimulate all the cells in your body and carry away the waste products that are related to fatigue. For the blood to do its work properly, it has to be fully charged with oxygen and to reject waste gases. Your overall health relies on the efficiency of your breathing.

If you tell someone to take a deep breath, nine times out of ten they will lift their chest high and raise their shoulders, arching the upper back. This is only using the upper part of the lungs. The Body Control method teaches you to use your thoracic and back muscles to enable you to expand the chest and ribs fully.

Try this simple exercise. It will give you some idea of exactly which muscles we want you to use.

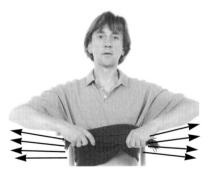

Sit or stand and wrap a towel around your ribs, crossing it over at the front.

Holding each opposite end of the towel and pulling it gently tight, breathe in and allow your ribs to expand the towel. As you breathe out, you may gently squeeze the towel to help you to empty your lungs fully and relax the rib cage.

Watch you do not lift the breastbone too high. This lateral, or thoracic breathing greatly improves the effectiveness of your overall breathing.

The rhythm of the breathing is also important. Each exercise has its own breathing pattern, which may vary according to which muscle the exercise is targeting. For most exercises, the rule is:

■ Breathe in to prepare for movement
■ Breathe out as you move.

Moving on the exhalation will enable you to relax into the stretch and prevent you from tensing up. It also safeguards against you holding your breath, which can unduly stress the heart and lead to serious complications later on.

At first, you may find it difficult to co-ordinate your breathing with your movements. Persevere for the end results are well worth it!

6 Flowing movements

'The attainment and maintenance of a uniformly developed body with a sound mind fully capable of naturally, easily and satisfactorily performing our many and varied daily tasks with spontaneous zest and pleasure.'

JOSEPH PILATES' DEFINITION OF
PHYSICAL FITNESS

Movement is a sign of life. As children we are comfortable and balanced in our bodies. We relish movement because we learn from it. As we grow older, however, our framework starts to suffer from various stresses. We no longer take the opportunity to move. Thérèse Bertherat in her book *The Body Has Its Reasons* (on the Mezières Method) likens it to having the potential to use all 26 letters of the alphabet and then only using words composed of the first five! From as young as five years of age, children are made to sit still and stop fidgeting – and yet fidgeting is far more natural than being cramped over a desk! When did you last jump for joy or skip just for the fun of it? Our bodies miss this spontaneous freedom. Injuries occur when we try to relive our youth or take up a sport, because we have not maintained our fitness.

The exercises in Body Control are designed to take you through a wide range of movements, in particular those you would not encounter in your normal daily activities. The movements are performed in a controlled manner to restore the health, enabling you to leap and skip safely should you wish to! As you move the body in ways it is not used to, you may find that you experience a feeling of releasing some emotion. Because we experience things with our bodies, it stands to reason that our bodies store those memories. When we move the muscles they can sometimes release those stored emotions. This is an important part of the healing process.

Spine Curls

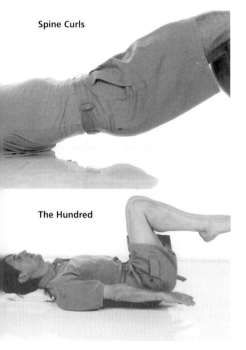

The Hundred

All the exercises have their own pace and rhythm. Some are performed very slowly (such as 'Spine Curls' – Exercise 12), while others require you to move parts of the body quite quickly ('The Hundred' – Exercise 24). However, none of your movements should ever be rushed or hurried, and all demand that you move smoothly and evenly. If you perform a movement hurriedly, you are more likely to cause damage and create tension – the 'high' you can get from an aerobic workout will often disguise such damage. This is also why, in Body Control, we prefer to work only to quiet background

music. If you are bouncing around to a fast beat, you are not listening to your body! Furthermore, if you move a muscle too quickly – by bouncing, for example – you risk bringing the 'stretch reflex' into effect. Muscle is like elastic and it behaves the same way in that, if you pull it sharply, it will 'twang' and shorten not lengthen. This achieves the exact opposite of what you actually are trying to achieve. It is far better to stretch slowly and relax into it, for the muscle then has the time to lengthen. Furthermore, if you move jerkily you risk jarring into the joints and damaging them.

Often it is far harder to perform a movement slowly than quickly. It is also less easy to cheat! In the absence of a teacher you must be honest with yourself and realize that working too quickly and carelessly will do you no good.

It is possible for energy to flow in two general directions: inwards towards the centre, which happens when muscles contract, or outwards, away from the centre, as when you reach or stretch. **Concentrate on flowing and lengthening outwards from a strong centre.**

7 Centring

The creation of a strong centre from which to begin is the focal point of the Body Control technique. It is a starting point for each exercise. We are aiming for what Joseph Pilates called a 'girdle of strength'. There are sound anatomical reasons for this, which are easy to see once you understand the relationship between the abdominal muscles and the spine.

The abdominal muscles act as a support for the spine and your internal organs. They form a natural corset, criss-crossing the torso in layers, thus preventing a vertebra from shearing forward off the vertebra below.

The Rectus Abdominis, the External and the Oblique muscles and the Tranversus Abdominis all have a role to play in supporting the middle. They are not designed simply to flex or bend the trunk – they have a postural role. The star player, however, is the Tranversus Abdominis, a deep abdominal muscle often ignored by other exercise

programmes. This muscle, in particular, has recently been the subject of much research* and has been proven to be crucial in the stabilization of the lumbar spine. This is in conjunction (co-contraction) with the Multifidus muscle, which is part of the Erector Spinae group. Any weakness in these two muscles will have an effect on the stability of your lower back.

We are aiming to improve the endurance of these key muscles. In all the exercises, whether lying, sitting or standing, we refer repeatedly to creating a firm and strong stomach. We ask you to locate and isolate the lower abdominals and to draw them up and in toward your spine. We are aiming for a mattress button effect between the navel and the spine. This is the starting point for most of the exercises – 'centring' involves stabilizing the torso and enabling you to safely lengthen and stretch, with your lower back protected. It is also why we teach lateral breathing into the sides and back, rather than deep into the abdomen. If your lower abdomen is extended when you breathe in, you cannot centre with your abdominals and you have left your back unprotected.

In the course of a one-hour session of Body Control, you are effectively performing hundreds of stomach exercises – no wonder we are creating a girdle of strength!

Draw the lower abdominals back towards the spine

*See Bibliography for articles from the Department of Physiotherapy, University of Queensland, Australia

8 Stamina

The postural muscles of the body need stamina and endurance. We are aiming to build up the endurance of the 'core' postural muscles. As you become more acquainted with the technique you will soon find that a series of exercises you once thought exhausting and a strain will seem effortless. The change will be gradual but, providing you practise regularly, steady. Even though most of the exercises are non-aerobic, you will also notice an improvement in your physical and mental stamina. This is all due to the conditioning programme.

TO SUM UP THE EIGHT PRINCIPLES

1 Relaxation – approach the exercises in a relaxed manner. Do not tense your muscles. Relax into the movements, but do not collapse into them.

2 Concentration – to maintain control, concentrate on what you are trying to do. Use the images to help you achieve the correct movement.

3 Co-ordination – try to develop your sense of body awareness to help improve your co-ordination. Practice will help you refine the movements.

4 Alignment – be vigilant in maintaining correct placement of your body parts! Before you start to move, run a mental checklist on your alignment:

■ Remember the 'North to South', 'East to West' neutral position (page 20)

■ Always lengthen up through the spine
■ Check that your neck is long and released
■ Think 'feet'

5 Breathing – don't forget to breathe! Breathe as wide and full as you can.

Remember:
■ Breathe in to prepare
■ Breathe out as you move

6 Flowing movements – no jerky or hurried movements. Lengthen slowly outwards from a strong centre.

7 Centring – create that 'girdle of strength'. Draw the navel (and below) in and up to spine before you move.

8 Stamina – slowly build up your stamina and endurance. Don't push yourself too far too fast.

Know Thyself

If you walked into a Body Control or Pilates studio anywhere in the world, the teacher would initially talk to you about your general health and enquire after any injuries or problem areas. You would be asked 'What are you hoping to achieve?'; 'What is your level of commitment?'; 'How long can you spend each week on exercising?' He or she would also ask about your hobbies, sport or work, to see if it involved lifting or bending, for example, or a repetitive action. Only when he or she has put together a complete portfolio of your lifestyle would the teacher cast a critical eye over you, assessing your posture, freedom of movement, state of tension, checking for any obvious imbalances.

Of course, the chances are that most of you reading this book will not yet have a Pilates or Body Control studio near you. So you will have to assess yourself.

On a scale of one to ten, how fit do you think you are?

1   10

Unfit   **Very Fit**

If you put '6', ask yourself why '6' and not '10'? Then ask yourself why '6' and not '1'?

How do you spend your days? Think about the actions you make each day – is there a pattern? Perhaps you can understand why you are tense in the shoulders or tight in the back?

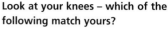
Stand in front of a mirror and ask yourself the following questions:

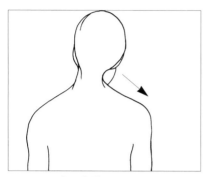

Does your head tilt to one side?

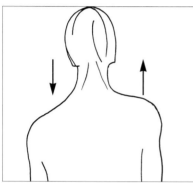

Are your shoulders level, or is one shoulder higher than the other?

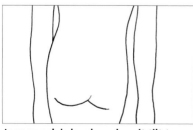

Is your pelvis level, or does it tilt to one side?

Look at your knees – which of the following match yours?

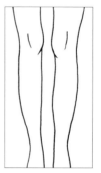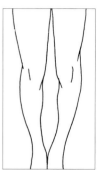

Cross-eyed knees   **Bow legs**

Knock knees   **Sway Back or Hyper-extended legs**

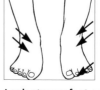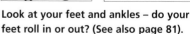

Look at your feet and ankles – do your feet roll in or out? (See also page 81).

If you noticed that your head was tilted, your shoulders were uneven and your pelvis was not level, you may have a lateral curvature of the spine or Scoliosis. Please turn to page 125.

We are all different shapes and sizes – and quite rightly, so for we inherit

Does your abdomen protrude?

Is your lower back markedly hollow or is it very flat? (See pages 124–5)

Is your head markedly forward? Are your shoulders rounded? (See page 124.)

Do you lean back? (See page 125, 'Sway Back'.)

different genetic characteristics. It is often hard to tell if your lower spine is over-arched or if you simply have a large derrière. However, the checklist above will give a rough idea of your body shape. It may help to stand with your back to a wall, so as to get a better idea of the curvature.

Compare this to the ideal on page 19 without being judgemental – it will give you a goal to aim for.

Body Control can help you to achieve your full potential, but we cannot alter your original bone structure. Large bones remain large, with or without exercise. At best, we can help you to achieve your full height and your optimum shape!

The last chapter of this book ('The Correction of Common Postural Faults', pages 124–5) contains several 'postural types' and guidelines as to which exercises are recommended for each body shape. Very few of us fall into one category and, for the reasons given above, it is not always easy to decide which is your type. If you are uncertain, you may be able to discuss this with your medical practitioner who can advise you.

Ready to Start

What do you need?

The best time to exercise is in the late afternoon or evening when your muscles are already warmed up as a result of the day's activity. Exercising in the morning is fine but you need to take longer to warm up carefully.

You may like to listen to a piece of classical music to help you relax.

Wear something warm and comfortable allowing for free movement – certainly not shoes! You may choose to wear non-slip socks or, better still, to go barefoot.

You will need:

■ peace and warmth. Put the answering machine on, or take the telephone off the hook
■ a thick mat or blanket to lie on. Please do not attempt to do the exercises on just the carpet, as you could hurt your spine. Unfortunately, a bed is too soft!
■ space to work in – you cannot keep stopping to move furniture out of the way. Some clear wall space is also useful
■ a small flat, but firm pillow for behind your head or perhaps a folded towel
■ a larger firm pillow, if you suffer from any neck problems
■ a pole, broomstick or stick of bamboo
■ a scarf – of the long variety
■ a tennis ball

Weights

There is a series of exercises which are weight-bearing. These exercises can be done without weights, or else you can very easily improvise – try using a tin of beans or a bag of rice or sugar for the arm exercises. There is even no reason why you couldn't strap a bag of rice to your ankles! If you are going to buy weights, be careful to buy the correct weight. Usually the weight given on the outside of the packaging is the combined weight of both hand or leg weights, so that a 1.4kg (3lb) pair will be 675g (1.5lb) each. Refer to the introduction of the 'Working with Weights' section (page 98) for our guidelines on weights.

For how long and how often should you exercise?

You will need to be honest and realistic with yourself about how often, and for how long, you can exercise. If you set yourself too high a goal, you will feel guilty if you fail to meet it. Alternatively, you may push yourself too hard and burn out. It is far better to start gently and build up as and when you feel you are ready. If you enjoy the programme, you will always manage to find the time, but there may have to be some sacrifices. There are only so many hours in the day, and work and family make important demands that have to be met for your own peace of mind. It will be no good trying to exercise if you are worried about the urgent fax you should be sending, or the dinner you haven't yet shopped for!

Having said all this, the more you practise, the greater the benefits will be. We should point out, by the way, that the work with weights should only be done for a maximum of three times per week and no more or you risk overusing the muscles.

As a guideline, a minimum of three sessions a week is recommended, with sessions building up to one hour in length. It is far, far better to do five exercises properly than to do fifteen exercises in a sloppy manner.

When should you not exercise?

Do not exercise:
■ if you are feeling at all unwell, as it is counter-productive
■ if you have just eaten a heavy meal
■ if you have been drinking alcohol
■ if you are in pain from an injury – consult your practitioner first, as rest may be needed before you exercise
■ if you have taken pain killers, as it will mask any warning pains
■ if you are undergoing medical treatment or taking drugs; you will need to consult your medical practitioner first

Remember, it is always wise to consult your doctor before you take up a new exercise regime, and always stop an exercise if it causes pain. Although many of these exercises are fine for use in pregnancy, we cannot recommend that you follow them as we have not designed the book with pregnancy in mind.

How to use the book
We have planned the book so that you can see easily what you are trying to achieve with each of the exercises.

Each left-hand page of the open book will tell you:
■ the aim of the exercise
■ the main muscles you are targeting and this really is only the main muscles, for to list all the muscles would be impossible. Often the muscles used to stabilize the body while a movement takes place elsewhere are equally important
■ images to help you to perform the exercise correctly
■ reminders of the 'Eight Principles'
■ 'Watchpoints' to look for. These are the sort of things that a teacher would be looking for in a Pilates class
■ warnings, where appropriate.

You must read the left-hand page before attempting the exercise on the opposite page – there is one exception, this being Exercise 4, 'Relaxation Position' (page 36).

When you have read the left-hand page, read the right-hand page several times – this page takes you through the exercise itself. It is always better to have an idea of where an exercise will take you before you start!

Always adhere to the 'Starting Position' and, when comfortable, follow the 'Action' section.

We are not expecting you to work through all the exercises in the same order each time. In the beginning, aim to learn only a few exercises per session.

Of course, as you become familiar with the exercises you won't need to read through the left-hand page each time. Please remind yourself constantly of the 'Watchpoints', however.

Always do the 'Warm-up' and 'Wind-down' exercises and then you can choose a selection from the other exercises.

At the back of the book ('Working Out with Body Control'), page 118, you will find suggestions for different times and combinations of exercises to ensure that you work out in a balanced way.

A word about the breathing – at first you will probably find the breathing very difficult. Please persevere as the breathing is an integral part of the exercise. But, it takes time to perfect, so be patient; take things one step at a time, and the breathing will come ...

The most important thing of all is to keep breathing – do not hold your breath. If you get confused halfway through an exercise, just breathe normally.

I consider Pilates to be an excellent form of exercise. Not only does it help focus the mind and 'centre' the body, it is ideal for specific reasons too. As a dancer, Pilates helps to strengthen, stretch and tone; as a singer, Pilates helps to correct posture and breathing; and if I am ever injured and unable to train fully, Pilates helps to maintain fitness while I am recuperating and repairing. I am a tremendous Pilates fan and fully appreciate the benefits it can bring!

BONNIE LANGFORD

The Warm-up

EXERCISE 1

Standing at Ease

Aim: to learn to stand in an easy and balanced way.

 Is this the future that awaits us all?

When you see someone with 'good posture' they look confident, composed, at ease with both themselves and their surroundings.

We inherit certain characteristics from our parents – the framework, the bones, the ligaments and the muscles. But it is how we use our bodies that determines our posture. Lack of physical activity, illnesses and injuries, mental and emotional outlook, mechanical stresses in the workplace and poor nutrition all have an effect on our posture. It is essentially bad postural habits that do most damage, and with the right level of awareness we can learn to control these.

We will be working on all the postural muscles in the exercises, but certain key muscles will be particularly targeted.

A word of warning!
Don't try too hard or you will create tension. We are aiming for a natural, balanced stance which is free from tension, enabling the spine to be long, the

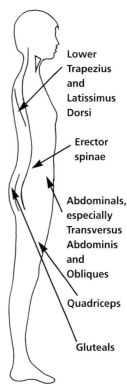

Lower Trapezius and Latissimus Dorsi

Erector spinae

Abdominals, especially Transversus Abdominis and Obliques

Quadriceps

Gluteals

shoulders to relax, the neck to be free, all the joints to be released. Yes, we ask you to use your abdominals to support your spine – but gently! Don't grip or your hips will lock up. You must stay flexible as you cannot hold good posture – it is dynamic. Think of the willow and the oak…we all know which survives the storm.

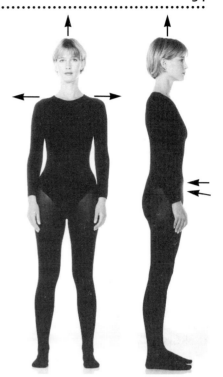

READ INSTRUCTIONS FROM THE BOTTOM UP:

12. Imagine someone has taken hold of the top of your head and is lengthening your spine up to the ceiling.

11. Aim for your chin to be parallel to the floor. Don't let it tilt forward (this will give you a double chin) or back (you will shorten the muscles at the back of your neck).

10. Allow the neck to release so that it can lengthen.

9. Don't pull the shoulders back, just let the arms hang from the shoulder sockets. They will naturally hang a little forward … don't force them back at all.

8. Allow the upper shoulders to soften, and keep giving directions throughout to relax and release them so as to stop any tension from forming.

7. Soften the breastbone and allow the back to widen.

6. Imagine that there is a tiny weight attached to your tailbone – allow it to help you to lengthen the base of the spine downwards. You don't want to tuck under, just

lengthen down. Remember the 'North to South' neutral position.

5. Create a long, strong centre by drawing the navel and below back to the spine.

4. Release the thigh muscles.

3. Keep the legs straight, but never locked. Soften the knees.

2. The weight should be evenly balanced in the centre of both feet (a triangle from the base of the big toe to the base of the small toe to the centre of the heel).

1. Stand in front of a mirror, if possible. Stand with your feet one hip-width apart and in parallel to each other.

EXERCISE 2
Roll-downs Against the Wall

Aim: increase both flexibility and strength in the spine. Learn how to use the abdominals to protect the spine. Release tension in the back and aid relaxation. You are also working the thigh muscles.

A wonderfully rejuvenating exercise, roll-downs really make you feel great and can be done almost anywhere – all you need is a wall!

They are especially useful if you are a back pain sufferer who is nervous of bending forward. If you prefer, you may slide your hands down your knees to give you a greater sense of stability.

The exercise can also be performed sitting in a straight-backed chair.

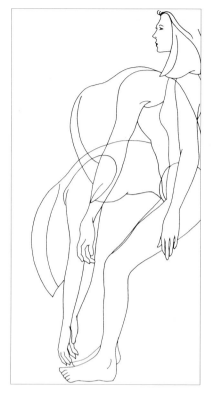

Think of the spine as a wheel. Try to peel the spine off the wall, bone by bone. As you come back up, drop the tailbone down, rotate the pelvis and place each vertebrae on the wall one-by-one…

'In coming up and going down, roll your spine like a wheel. Vertebra by vertebra, try to roll and unroll.'
JOSEPH PILATES

Watchpoints:
✔ Keep the feet in parallel.
✔ Keep the neck and head relaxed until you are completely upright.
✔ Remember to draw the navel back to the spine throughout.

STARTING POSITION
Stand with your feet about 46 centimetres (18 inches) from a wall, one hip-width apart and in parallel. Lean back into the wall bending the knees – if viewed from the side, you will look as though you are sitting on a high stool. Don't try to take the head back onto the wall.

4. Slowly start to roll forward, peeling the spine off the wall. Your arms and hands are relaxed. Your neck and head stay relaxed and your bottom remains on the wall. Only go so far as you are comfortable but aim to reach the floor eventually. You may bend your knees further if it is more comfortable.

★ACTION
1. Breathe in to prepare for movement, lengthen up through the spine.

2. As you start to breathe out, gently draw the navel back to the spine – it will take the small of your back closer to the wall. (If you have a large derrière you may not feel this.)

3. Still breathing out, allow the chin to drop forward by letting go of the head and neck, to feel as if your forehead is weighted.

5. As you hang, breathe in.

6. Breathe out as you draw the navel to the spine and, rotating the pelvis, bring the pubic bone toward the chin. Slowly, bone by bone, curl your spine back onto the wall as you come up.

7. Remember to breathe out as you move the spine.

REPEAT SIX TIMES.

EXERCISE 3
Sliding Down the Wall

Aim: to learn how to lengthen the base of the spine, achieving the correct angle of the pelvis to the spine. This exercise works the thigh muscles and stretches the Achilles' Tendon.

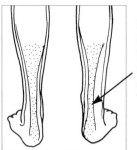

Leaving the heels down helps to stretch the Achilles' Tendon.

This exercise has the advantage that you are able to practise it anywhere, even where space is limited.

To achieve good posture it is essential that the pelvis is at the correct angle to the spine. This is a wonderful way to learn to lengthen the base of the spine but without over-tilting the pelvis or 'tucking under' too far.

Always remember 'North to South' (page 20).

Refer back to the section on Alignment (page18) if you need any extra help.

Remember that we are aiming for a neutral position with the back neither arched nor flat, but rather with the natural curves of the spine lengthened and supported with strong abdominal muscles.

This exercise has the added advantage of strengthening the thigh muscles. If you have back problems it is vital that these muscles remain strong so that you may bend your knees and squat while you lift heavy objects!

IN SEARCH OF THE CORRECT PELVIC ANGLE:

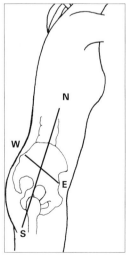

Wrong

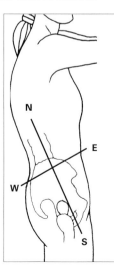

Wrong

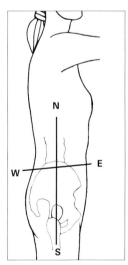

Right

Watchpoints:
✔Watch that you don't slide too far down (never take your bottom below knee level).
✔Check that your knees are passing directly over your feet and not inside them. Your feet must stay parallel, don't let them roll inwards.
✔Keep your heels on the floor.
✔Remember do not allow your tailbone to lift off the wall.

Note: If you have a large derrière, you will not be able to feel the small of your back on the wall.

STARTING POSITION
Stand, back to the wall, with your feet about 15 centimetres (6 inches) away from the wall. Your feet are hip-width apart and parallel.
Lean back into the wall. Don't try to force your head back onto the wall, just stand there comfortably.
Before you begin, take note as to which parts of your back are touching the wall.

★ACTION
1. Breathe in to prepare.

2. Breathe out and draw the navel back to the spine and wall.

3. Bend your knees and slide about 30 centimetres (12 inches) down the wall until your thighs are almost parallel with the floor – don't go any lower than this! You should now notice that your back is lengthened. Keep your feet flat on the floor (your heels will want to come up – don't let them). Don't allow your tailbone to lift off the wall, rather keep it lengthening out away from you.

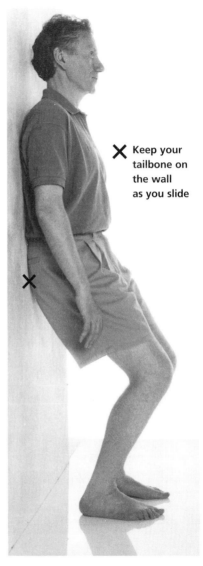

✗ **Keep your tailbone on the wall as you slide**

4. Breathe in as you slide back up, still trying to keep the base of the spine lengthened.

REPEAT EIGHT TIMES.

As you leave the wall, stand upright for a moment imagining that the wall is still there.

EXERCISE 4

Relaxation Position

It is better to do the exercise first and then to read this page.

Aim: to develop body awareness. Release the lower back into the floor, so lengthening the spine. To lengthen the neck and to relax the upper back allowing it to widen. And to release any areas where there may be tension.

This is an exercise in awareness and, as such, you are doing very little – you are, however, thinking and feeling. The end position is perfect for relaxation, being far better than just lying down – we hope the exercise proves this. It is also the starting position for many of the exercises to follow.

While you are in lying flat out, you probably made the following observations about your body:

Your chest may be lifted

Your neck is shortened	Your back may be arched	Your knees are pressed down

When you have rearranged yourself into the next position, you will hopefully feel that your body, especially your back, is far more comfortable. This position allows the spine to lengthen naturally, giving it the opportunity to recover from the effects of gravity and poor posture,

which combine together to compress the spine.

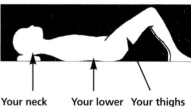

Your neck can lengthen and release	Your lower back can release	Your thighs can release. The hips can open

Lengthening the spine is very important. The curves of the spine are there for a reason as, quite simply, without them you would fall over! We are not trying to lose the natural curves, but poor posture leads to the curves becoming exaggerated – and it is in those sections of the spine where the curves are greatest that the weaknesses lie. It is in these areas that you are most likely to injure yourself.

On the opposite page we have given you a relaxation exercise. Obviously, how long you can spend in this position will depend on how long you have set aside for your workout. We would not expect you to relax for a long period if you are doing the daily sessions set out in 'Working Out with Body Control' (page 118). The aim is to relax, centre yourself and increase your awareness before continuing with the exercises. You may like to do this relaxation at the end of the workout session as well.

EQUIPMENT
■ A small, flat, firm pillow

PREPARATION
Lie on your back with your legs extended on the floor. Your arms are by your side, with your head resting on the floor.

Take notice as to which parts of your body are touching the floor.

Notice if your lower back is arching off the floor.

Notice the curve of your neck and of your ankle.

Imagine you are lying in warm, wet sand – what imprint would your body make?

STARTING POSITION
Now bring your knees up to a bent position, one at a time. Your feet are flat on the floor, one hip-width apart.

Place a small flat and firm pillow behind your head so that your face is now lying parallel to the floor – you may need someone to check this for you. The chin should be neither tucked forward nor tilted back – see the photograph below.

Bring your hands so that they are resting on your abdomen, with the elbows open and wide.

★ACTION
1. Allow the floor to support you. Note which parts of your body now touch the floor.

2. Allow your feet to lengthen and widen, the toes are long.

3. Relax the calf muscles, imagine the knees are suspended from the ceiling by a rope – release the thighs.

4. Open the hip joints.

5. Take your awareness to the lower back, soften the front of the pelvis to release the lower back into the floor, as if you are lying in a hammock.

6. Try to release your upper back into the floor by softening the breastbone and the front of the shoulders. Allow the back to widen with each out-breath, with the shoulders melting into the floor.

7. Your neck is naturally long, with the top of your head lengthening away.

8. Check that your jaw isn't clenched. Allow your tongue to widen at its base and to rest comfortably in the bottom of your mouth.

Relaxed position

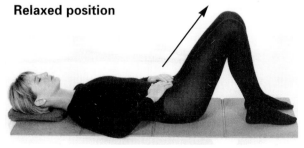

9. Your eyes are gently closed. Allow the forehead to be wide, smooth and free of lines. Relax into gravity and observe your breath without interrupting it.

EXERCISE 5

Breathing Correctly

Aim: to learn lateral or thoracic breathing, involving proper use of the lungs and expansion of the ribcage.

We have already discussed the importance of correct breathing and, as you know, Body Control teaches lateral or thoracic breathing (see page 20). There are several reasons for this. Consider the positioning of the lungs themselves. They are situated in the ribcage. Most people breathe too 'shallowly', moving only the upper part of the chest and denying the lungs their full expansion.

When you breathe in, a large dome-shaped muscle called the diaphragm lowers and the rib cage opens and expands laterally, permitting the lungs to draw in air like a pump. As you breathe out, the diaphragm rises and the ribcage closes and contracts which, in turn, aids the expulsion of air from the lungs.

As the diaphragm lowers, there is naturally some movement in the abdomen. To restrict it would prevent the lungs from fully expanding in all directions.

A word of warning though – the deliberate throwing-out of the lower abdominals, which unfortunately is how most people interpret deep breathing, is counterproductive during exercise (the deep abdominal breath used by yogis is a different matter!). If your lower abdominals are extended with air, you will have left your lower-back unprotected and vulnerable to injury, particularly when you are doing an exercise such as the 'Single Leg Stretch' (Exercise 23, page 74).

We are aiming to give the lungs as much space as possible to expand, thereby widening the upper body, filling the sides and back (see also Exercise 30, 'Rest Position', page 96).

Equally important to achieving a full breath is the lengthening of the upper spine, which allows the ribs to open out, moving freely, gently massaging the muscles and encouraging them to release.

Watchpoints:
✔Do not force the 'in' breath, just allow it to happen naturally.
✔It is possible to 'over-breathe', especially in the very beginning. Look for signs of light-headedness or dizziness – this is simply caused by an overdose of oxygen reaching the blood. Our bodies are not used to so much of a good thing!
✔If you feel queasy, stop and take time out. Your body will soon adapt and benefit from correct breathing – just give it time.

STARTING POSITION
Lie in the relaxation position as described in Exercise 4.
Place your hands gently on the sides of your lower ribcage.

★ACTION
1. As you breathe in, allow the breath to expand the lungs, ribs and back, filling your sides like bellows. Your fingers should separate.

2. As you breathe out, allow the ribs to close down, the upper body to deflate and your breastbone to soften, with tension between the shoulder blades seeping away down into the floor.

3. Allow the 'out' breath to be as full and complete as possible.

4. Don't force the 'in' breath because, with a complete 'out' breath, the air will naturally flood in to fill your lungs.

REPEAT FOR EIGHT BREATHS.

EXERCISE 6
Navel to Spine

Aim: to learn how to use the abdominals, especially the Tranversus Abdominis muscle, to protect the lumbar spine. Learn how to lengthen the lumbar spine and the correct placement of the pelvis and spine in a neutral position.

The creation of a strong centre is a primary goal in Body Control. The centre is the starting point to all the exercises, from which you can safely stretch or strengthen.

Centring also enables you to take advantage of the centre of gravity for the body – this lies just behind the navel, at the very front of the spine, by the third or fourth lumbar vertebra.

The instruction to draw the navel to the spine is always coupled with the instruction to lengthen the spine. The two go hand in hand, for an elongated spine supported by strong abdominals is paramount.

It is important, however, that you do not tuck under too far, lifting the bottom off the floor. Neither should you push your spine down or grip tightly with the

muscles around your hips. Remember the 'North to South' neutral position on page 20 – this will help you to achieve the correct placement.

Once you start to move your limbs, you will need to work your abdominals a little harder. Note, however, that during the more strenuous exercises, especially whenever the legs are raised, you will need to draw the muscles back and in firmly to anchor the spine to the mat, preventing it from arching off the floor. Here, as well, you will need to keep the navel back to the spine for both the 'in' and 'out' breath. In order to do this, you must breathe laterally.

Learning to use only the necessary amount of contraction in a muscle to do the job comes with time and practice.

—The centre

Watchpoints:
✔Do not over-grip the stomach muscles – hollow them and hold.
✔The tailbone should remain on the floor, lengthening away. Don't tuck under.
✔As you lengthen the arms and legs away, try not to let the back arch.

STARTING POSITION
Lie on your back with your knees bent, feet one hip-width apart and parallel. Your arms are resting on your lower abdomen. The head is resting on a small, flat, firm pillow if necessary.

★ACTION 1
1. Before you start the exercise, find your neutral spine position – refer to the exercise on page 20 to help. You need to gently tilt the pelvis up to the navel (North), then tilt it towards your pubic bone (South).

2. Now find the level neutral position between the two. The compass pointer is like a spirit level.

3. Maintaining this neutral position, breathe in to prepare.

4. As you breathe out, soften the front of your pelvis, allowing the area of the navel and lower abdominals to hollow out towards the spine. Imagine that you are lying in a hammock. Hold the abdominals in this hollowed position. At the same time, feel how your lumbar spine lengthens.

5. Breathe in and relax.

REPEAT FIVE TIMES.

★ACTION 2
1. Breathe in to prepare.

2. As you start to breathe out, hollow out the lower abdominals, drawing the navel back to the spine, feel the abdominals wrapping themselves around your middle like a corset. Lengthen the tailbone away, but keep it on the floor.

3. Still breathing out, slide the right leg away along the floor and take the right arm above your head to touch the floor behind.

4. Enjoy the stretch from your fingertips to your toes. Do not allow the back to arch – try to keep the navel back to the spine.

5. Breathe in as you return the arm and leg to the starting position.

REPEAT WITH THE LEFT ARM AND LEG.

REPEAT FIVE TIMES TO EACH SIDE.

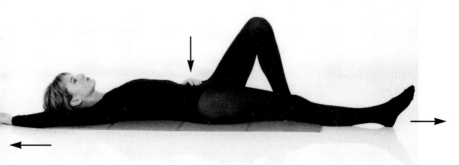

EXERCISE 7
Knee Circles & Leg Circles

Aim: Knee Circles: to mobilize your hip joints and to keep them free. Learn how to work your leg while keeping your torso firmly anchored and stable. Leg Circles: as for Knee Circles, but now you are also toning your thigh muscles.

Healthy joints means joints that are open, well lubricated, mobile and able to move easily through their complete range. Hip-replacement operations are now one of the most common orthopaedic procedures. Without movement, a joint can seize up. These two exercises are designed to stop that happening.

Finding your hip joint
Do you know where your hip joint is? If you were to draw a line from your knee to your groin, you would arrive at the hip joint. Lift your leg upwards, bending your knee while doing so, feel the point where the movement originates – this is the hip joint.

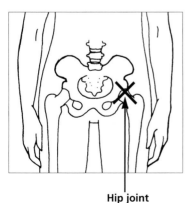

Hip joint

The hip joint is a ball and socket joint which allows for a wide range of movement. Think of it as a ball bearing! As you circle and stir the leg, open it, release it, and enjoy its freedom.

Watchpoints:
✔Don't take the leg too wide at the beginning of the exercise or you will rock from side to side. It is far better to keep the circle small and the torso calm and firmly anchored. For this exercise, remember to maintain a balance between East and West.
✔ 'Check your neck' – don't let it arch back, keep it long and soft.
✔ Watch that you keep your shoulders relaxed.
✔Holding the scarf from underneath, palms towards you, can help you to keep the shoulder blades down and anchored to the floor.
✔ Breathe normally throughout both exercises.
✔ Keep your tailbone down on the floor throughout.

EQUIPMENT
■ An ordinary scarf

Knee Circles
STARTING POSITION
Lie on your back with your knees bent. Feet should be hip-width apart and parallel. Place a small, flat, firm pillow beneath your head if necessary.

★ACTION
1. Bring one knee up towards your chest so that it is directly above your hip. Place a scarf around the lower part of the thigh, holding an end of the scarf in each hand – have the palm facing towards you as you hold the scarf. Keep your elbows open.

2.Use your lower abdominals to keep the pelvis stable – not allowing it to rock from side to side – gently and slowly rotate the bent leg around. Do this five times clockwise, then five times anti-clockwise. As you do so, think of releasing the thigh bone from the hip socket. Allow the scarf (and your hands) to help move the leg. Breathe normally as you move the leg.

REPEAT WITH THE OTHER LEG.

When you have mastered keeping the pelvis still while circling the knee, try the following exercise.

Leg Circles
STARTING POSITION
The same position as for Knee Circles but this time no scarf is required.

★ACTION
1. Straighten one leg up into the air. The foot is softly pointed. You may keep the knee slightly bent to begin with, but ultimately you want to have the leg fully straightened. When you can easily straighten the leg, flex the foot. (For advice or pointing and flexing, see page 84–5). The other foot remains on the floor, with the knee bent.

2. Keeping the pelvis calm and stable and the tailbone down, rotate the leg slowly around in a circle – five times clockwise, then five times anti-clockwise. Make sure the foot is relaxed, unless you are doing the advanced version.

REPEAT WITH THE OTHER LEG.

EXERCISE 8

Hamstring Stretch

Aim: to stretch the hamstrings while keeping the torso stable, the back anchored and without creating any tension elsewhere in the body.

The hamstrings are, in fact, a group of three muscles, so called because in past times farmers would sever the hamstrings of pigs to prevent them from wandering away!

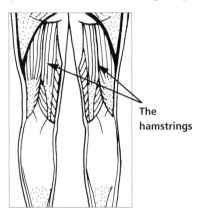

The hamstrings

The hamstrings flex and bend the knee. We spend far too much time sitting and, as a result, the hamstrings don't get the natural stretching they need. Most of us have suffered the agony of painful hamstrings after a return to exercise or an over-vigorous exercise session. There is much debate as to which exercise is best for the hamstrings. Some will bring results quicker but, at the same time, carry a greater risk of injury. The exercise most commonly given to stretch them is the forward bend. 'Careless' forward bending with straight legs can, however, can put enormous pressure on the low back

and knees with disastrous results. It is far better to stretch a little and often, gently easing out the muscles rather than pulling on them. Have you ever tried to undo a knot in a piece of cotton by tugging at it?

Why do we need to stretch the hamstrings?
Short, tight hamstrings can affect your whole posture. They will pull the back of the pelvic bowl downwards causing the lower back to flatten.

If your hamstrings are too short, they will greatly restrict your flexibility and increase the risk of damage being caused to the lumbar spine in everyday forward bending or sport.

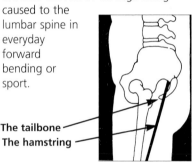

The tailbone
The hamstring

Watchpoints:
✔ Don't allow the pelvis to twist as you straighten the leg – anchoring navel to spine will help you. North to South. East to West (see page 34).
✔ **Keep your tailbone (coccyx) down** as you stretch the leg.
✔ 'Check your neck' – often the neck shortens and arches back as the hamstrings are stretched. If this happens, place a small, flat, firm pillow under your head to keep the neck long. Think of softening the neck and breastbone and of opening the elbows. Hold the scarf as for 'Knee Circles' (Exercise 7, page 42) – it will encourage you to **keep the shoulder blades down and together.**
✔ Don't strain – ease the leg out, gently stretching it within your limits.

EQUIPMENT
■ Scarf

STARTING POSITION
Lie on your back with your knees bent, feet flat on the floor and one hip-width apart.

Use a small, flat, firm pillow if necessary. Many people arch their neck considerably with this exercise, so you may need a pillow here, even if this is not so for the other exercises.

Bring one knee toward your chest. Hold the scarf from underneath, with your palms towards you. Place the scarf over the sole of one foot.

★ACTION
1. Breathe in to prepare.

2. Breathe out as you anchor navel to spine, neutral 'North to South' positioning.

3. Slowly straighten the leg into the air, the foot being flexed downwards toward your face. Your tailbone stays down on the floor.

4. Breathing normally now, hold the stretch for the count of ten.

5. Relax the leg by gently bending it again.

REPEAT FIVE TIMES TO EACH LEG.

N ——— S

EXERCISE 9
Hip Flexors

Aim: to stretch and work the Hip Flexors (the 'psoas' muscle) and to learn how to bend the knee by hinging from the hip joint and without twisting the pelvis.

The psoas* muscle is responsible for flexing (bending) the knee onto the chest and flexing the trunk, that is, it makes it bend forward at the waist.

A tight psoas muscle has far reaching effects on the rest of the body. It actually attaches the lower spine to the thigh bone and if it is tight, which is very common, it upsets the placement of the pelvis on the spine causing the condition known as lordosis or 'hollow back'.

This exercise will help to stretch the psoas. If you find that you cannot straighten the leg along the floor without arching the back, then that is a fair indicator that your psoas is tight – although be aware that it can also be the result of a rather large bottom!

Think about dropping the top of the thigh bone down into the hip socket as you bend it onto your chest. This will stop you from overworking the psoas. The psoas will often overwork trying to stabilise the pelvis, at the expense of the deep core muscles. You need to learn how to release the psoas.

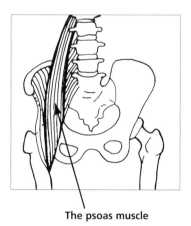

The psoas muscle

Watchpoints:
✔ Do not allow the back to arch. Remember 'North to South', neutral spine (see page 20).
✔ 'Check your neck' – don't let it shorten or tighten, keep it soft.
✔ Don't be tempted to merge knee-bending and leg-extending. Follow the instructions carefully as they are designed to give you maximum result and benefit.
✔ Don't allow the pelvis to twist.
✔ Keep your tailbone lengthening away.

*It in fact comprises three muscles.

STARTING POSITION
Lie on your back, with your knees
bent and feet flat on the floor.

★ACTION
1. Breathe in to prepare.

2. As you breathe out, hollow out
the lower abdominals, navel to
spine, and – keeping that sense of
hollowness in the pelvis – hinge
the right knee up to your chest,
dropping the thigh bone down
into the hip joint.

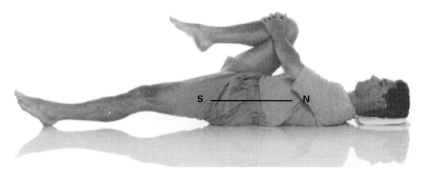

3. Breathe in as you clasp the
right leg below the knee (or
behind the lower part of the
thigh if you have joint problems).

4. Holding onto the leg, breathe
out as you extend the left leg
along the floor. Your lower back
should remain down. If it arches,
bend the left knee back up again.

5. Breathe in as you slide the left
leg back up into the starting
position.

6. Breathe out as you lower the
right bent knee to the floor,
keeping the sense of
hollowness in the abdomen.

**REPEAT WITH THE OTHER SIDE
FOR A TOTAL OF FIVE TIMES TO
EACH SIDE.**

EXERCISE 10
Shoulder Drops

Aim: to release any tension contained in the upper body, warming up the arms and shoulders.

We spend much of our day hunched forward and tense.

Stop reading for a moment and think about how much tension you have in your body. How are you holding this book? The chances are high that you are gripping it tightly with your shoulders hunched? Have you tightly crossed your legs or flexed your feet?

We all unwittingly hold on ... learning to let go is very difficult because first you have to be aware that you are holding tension. When you can spot it you are already halfway there. Then you have to let it release. The upper part of the shoulders can be particularly tense, because we tend to hunch ourselves over our work or while driving.

Watchpoints:
✔Don't roll too much from side to side.
✔ Make the movement come directly from the shoulder blade.
✔ Don't drop the elbow right back down to the floor – it can stay relaxed, yet still lifted towards the ceiling.

STARTING POSITION

Lie with your knees bent, and your feet one hip-width apart on the floor and flat. Keep your neck long – use a small, flat, firm pillow if it helps you. Raise both arms up to the ceiling, directly above your shoulders.

★ACTION

1. Breathe in as you reach one arm up to the ceiling, allowing the shoulder blade to come off the floor. Stretch right through to the finger tips.

2. Breathe out as you allow the whole shoulder to release down to the floor.

REPEAT WITH THE OTHER ARM.

THEN REPEAT TEN TIMES WITH EACH ARM ALTERNATELY.

EXERCISE 11
Neck Rolls
& Nose Spirals

Aim: to release tension from the neck and to learn the correct relationship between the neck and head.

The relationship between the neck and head are of great importance. Most of us are unaware of the fact that the spine actually begins between the ears.

The neck is very sensitive to stress and tension. This is due to a phenomenon known as the 'startle reflex' – this was nature's way of protecting the head and, therefore, the brain. It works like this ... when you are taken by surprise the muscles at the back of the neck shorten to tilt the head back defensively. Simply observe what happens to you if someone catches you unawares. The basic problem is that our modern lifestyle means that most of us are either permanently startled or under stress, so that the head is always held tilted back with the muscles are permanently shortened. This exercise should help you to release that tension.

Sometimes a neck problem originates from lower down in the spine. If you are locked in the thoracic area of the upper back this will throw the neck off

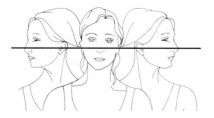

Roll the head on its axis.

balance. Similarly, if you hold tension in your jaw it can give you pain in your neck.

Remember that the body is a closed system – upset one area and the rest is thrown out of kilter. With both of these exercises you are aiming to release the neck. It is vital that you do not force the neck in any way, just let it roll.

We talk about a 'long neck', but keeping the neck long while exercising is really quite difficult. Most of us have the habit of arching the neck back as we work the rest of the body. 'Check your neck' is a watchpoint that occurs throughout the book. It would be equally harmful, however, to lock the neck down. Finding the right balance is the goal ...

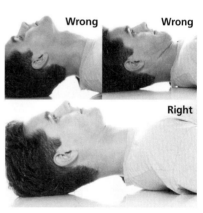

One final word about your neck – try to soften both the neck and the breastbone as you work, as it's amazing how often the neck joins in, when it's the abdominals that should be working!

Watchpoints:
✔ Do not force the neck. If you experience any tingling in the fingers, you are probably pinching a nerve. In this case, consult your medical practitioner before continuing.

✔ When executing nose spirals, make sure you move the whole head.

STARTING POSITION
Lie on your back with your knees bent, feet one hip-width apart and parallel, and flat on the floor.

If your chin is pointing backwards and your neck really arching back, use a small, flat, firm pillow or simply fold a towel into four, and lay it under your neck and head to bring the face into parallel with the floor.

Neck Rolls
★ACTION
1. Gently roll your head to the left – just let it be taken by its own weight.

2. Roll it back to the centre, and then over to the right.

3. Come back to the centre and then, very slowly, lift your chin to gently arch the neck to look behind you.

4. Come back to the centre and then, keeping the head on the floor, gently rotate the head forward bringing the chin towards the chest and lengthening the back of the neck. (Keep your head on the floor.)

5. Come back to the centre.

REPEAT THE SEQUENCE FIVE TIMES.

Nose Spiral
★ACTION
Close your eyes and, starting at the centre of an imaginary spiral, circle your nose, allowing the head to release as it gently rolls around. Gradually increase the size of the circles as your spiral grows. Then slowly start to spiral back towards the centre. Try to make the movement smooth and round … no square or jerky spirals please!

REPEAT THREE TIMES.

2

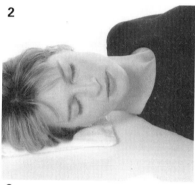

3

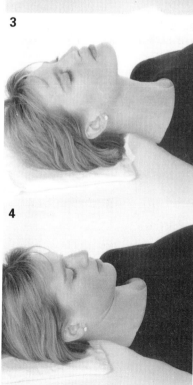

4

EXERCISE 12
Spine Curls

Aim: to mobilize the spine, releasing tension in the muscles around the spine and to strengthen the back and buttock muscles.

One of the most common causes of backache is a tight, inflexible spine. Frequently, several vertebra get 'locked' together – you might feel this as you attempt the exercise. They will move as a wedge, not separately. If one part of the spine locks, it will affect the movement and performance of the rest of the spine as each section is dependent on the mobility of the whole spine.

You are also learning to control each segment of the spine, working the deep muscles closely attached to it.

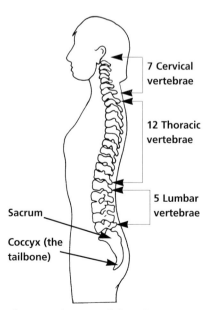

The natural curves of the spine.

7 Cervical vertebrae

12 Thoracic vertebrae

5 Lumbar vertebrae

Sacrum

Coccyx (the tailbone)

The discs
Did you know that you are taller in the morning than in the evening? The discs between each vertebra are wider when you wake before the effects of gravity, coupled with poor posture, combine to shorten them. They lose fluid as the day wears on and literally shrink. This is also the effect of ageing.

Think about putting 7.5 centimetres (three inches) between each bone as you lower your spine to the floor, lengthening the spine and increasing the space between each vertebra.

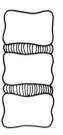 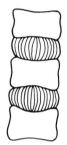

The discs are compressed by gravity.

The discs after resting and lengthening.

Visualize the spine moving smoothly like a wheel, peeling each vertebra off the floor bone by bone, and then wheeling it back.

Watchpoints:
✔ Don't allow the back to arch. Keep the tailbone tucked under like a whippet who's just been ticked off.
✔ Keep your feet in parallel, don't let them roll in or out. The weight should stay evenly balanced.
✔ Remember to peel the spine off bone by bone, separating each of them.
✔ 'Check your neck' – don't let it arch back, keep it long and soft.
✔ If your arms ache, bring them down by your sides again.

EQUIPMENT
■ A mat or a thick blanket

STARTING POSITION
Lie on your back on a mat or a thick blanket with your knees bent, your feet about 30 centimetres (twelve inches) from your buttocks.

Your feet should be one hip-width apart and parallel.

Take your arms above your head, resting them on the floor, a shoulder-width apart. If this is uncomfortable, then leave the arms by your side.

★ACTION
1. To prepare, breathe in.

2. Breathe out and hollow out the lower abdominal muscles down towards the spine.

3. Slowly and carefully, lift just the base of your spine (the coccyx, or tailbone) away from the floor.

4. Breathe in, breathe out as you lower and lengthen the spine back onto the floor.

5. Repeat, lifting a little more of the spine off the floor each time. As you lower, put down each part of the spine in sequence – bone by bone, aim to put 7.5 centimetres (three inches) between each vertebra – the back of the ribs, the waist, the small of the back - only when this is down do you lower and release the buttocks.

6. Make certain that your back does not arch – rather, keep the pubic bone directed towards your chin and the tailbone lengthening away.

DO FIVE OF THESE EXERCISES.

BREATHING
■ Breathe out as you raise the spine.
■ Breathe in whilst the spine is raised.
■ Breathe out as you slowly lower.

EXERCISE 13
Hip Rolls

Warning: If you have a low back problem check with your practitioner before doing this exercise.

Aim: to stretch the sides and back safely, while keeping the pelvis at the correct angle to the spine (not arching the back) and to work the waist. To lengthen the muscles on either side of the spine up into the rib cage, open the chest and work the abdominal muscles.

This is a fabulous stretch. The secret is to control the movement carefully, hence the use of the tennis ball. You will only get the full benefit of the stretch if you stop the legs from sliding apart. If you feel the ball rolling around, then you have gone too far!

Watchpoints:
✔ Keep the opposite shoulder firmly down on the floor.
✔ Keep the knees in line. Don't go too far unless you can control it.
✔ Use the abdominals at all times, feel as though you are moving the legs from the stomach.
✔ Don't twist up into the spine – it is a sideways lateral movement.

EQUIPMENT
■ Tennis ball
■ Hand weights (optional)

STARTING POSITION
Lie on your back, with your arms
out to the side and palms up.
Knees should be up towards your
chest, but in line with your hips.
Your thighs will be at right angles
to your body and your feet are
softly pointed.

Place the tennis ball between
your knees.

If you so wish, you can hold
weights in your hands to help
keep the shoulders down on the
floor.

★ACTION
1. Breathe in then, as you breathe
out, draw the navel back to the
spine and slowly lower your legs
toward the floor on your left side,
turning your head to the right.
Keep your right shoulder down on
the ground. Keep the knees in
line.

2. Breathe in and breathe out
again bringing the navel to the
spine. Use this strong centre to
bring your legs back to the
middle, while returning the head
to the middle.

3. Breathe in and then out, and
repeat the twisting movement to
the opposite side.

REPEAT TEN TIMES IN EACH
DIRECTION.

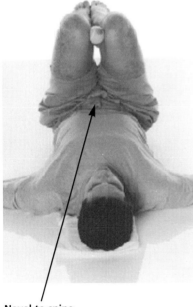

Navel to spine
throughout

I'd had enough of looking red and sweaty in a spandex leotard, so Pilates came as a relaxing, strengthening, graceful relief.

I'd started out as a muscley aerobicised 80s product, and ended up a slender, upright 90s swan – under Gordon's careful tutelage.

TRACY ULLMAN

Lengthening & Strengthening

EXERCISE 14
The Corkscrew

Aim: to learn to use the arms without creating tension in the upper shoulders and to open the front of the chest. Work between the shoulder blades while learning correct shoulder placement.

Very few of us are free from tension in the upper shoulders. Bent over a desk, cooker or driving in heavy traffic are all positions which encourage round shoulders and the build-up of tension. Add to this the stresses of everyday life and you are well on the way to getting a tension headache.

It is strange that, while many of the muscles in our bodies suffer from underuse, with the shoulders and neck the exact opposite is true – we overuse them. A muscle is either working or resting, contracting or releasing. And a muscle that is overtense is one that cannot rest or be released so it stays working, contracted beyond its needs and is never fully 'turned off'.

The long-term result of an overly tense muscle is the build-up of lactic

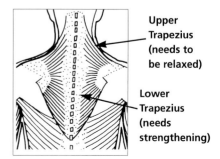

Upper Trapezius (needs to be relaxed)

Lower Trapezius (needs strengthening)

acid in the fibres. Usually lactic acid, which is a waste product of muscle activity, disappears naturally when the muscle relaxes. If the muscle does not relax however, the lactic acid builds up, causing injury to the tissue, and when the muscle is called upon to act again it cannot respond normally to the nervous instruction. It cannot reach its normal length when needed, and movement therefore becomes restricted. As the body is a closed system, this restriction of movement has a knock-on effect on the rest of the body.

The Upper Trapezius is the most common site for tension. We tense it when there is no need as a response to stress or when faced with an activity such as lifting the arms. While the Upper Trapezius overworks, the lower section is underused.

If you can let go of tension here, think of the energy you will save! It can used to better effect!

Think about dropping the upper shoulders down as the arms raise and moving the arms from the lower part of the shoulder blades.

Watchpoints:
✔ Remember not to arch the back as you bring your elbows back.
✔ Don't forget to drop the shoulders down – and keep them down.

STARTING POSITION
Stand correctly – balanced, with spine lengthened and navel to spine.

★ACTION
1. To prepare breathe in and lengthen up through the spine.

2. Breathe out as you allow your arms to almost float upwards. Keep the upper shoulders relaxed;

think of them dropping down as the arms raise. Clasp your hands lightly behind your head.

3. As you breathe in, shrug your shoulders up to your ears.

4. Breathe out as you drop them down. Breathe in as you gently bring your elbows back a little. Your shoulder blades will then come together.

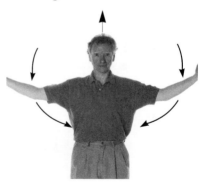

5. Breathe out as you release your hands and slowly bring them down by your side, opening them wide.

6. Allow the head, neck and spine to lengthen up as the arms come down – think of a corkscrew.

REPEAT THREE TIMES.

EXERCISE 15

The Samson

Aim: to open the upper back and to stretch the muscles of the hand, wrist and forearm. Focus on the shoulder joint. Achieve a morning-style stretch!

You can easily see where the exercise gets its name from. With the Samson, you are strengthening the muscles around the joint without stressing the joint itself. This is a crucial part of the Body Control technique, the developing of strong muscles to protect a joint, while affording its maximum range of movement. In order to achieve this, a smooth, controlled movement is often more effective than a wild, uncontrolled, large movement. Furthermore, after attempting the Samson, you will discover that it is often difficult to perform, as it requires precise control!

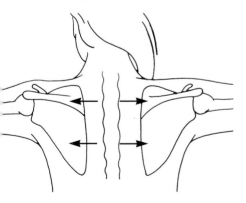

Keep opening and widening the upper back.

Watchpoints:

✔ Be careful not to hunch the shoulders up. Keep the neck relaxed and long, maintaining the distance between the ears and the shoulders.

✔ Keep lengthening the arms away, reaching out to the sides of the room.

✔ Should you feel any tingling in the fingers, lower the arms and rest before trying again. Build up slowly. If the tingling is troublesome, leave this exercise out.

✔ Keep reminding yourself of the 'Standing Instructions', lengthening the spine etc. (see page 31).

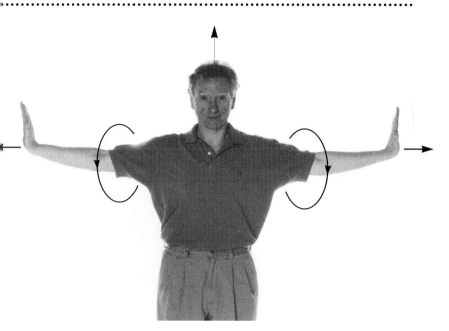

STARTING POSITION
Stand correctly, lengthening up through the spine.

Extend the arms to the side, so that they are positioned evenly with your shoulders.

★ACTION
1. Flex your hands as though you are pressing solidly against imaginary walls. The heels of your hands are lengthening out away from the shoulders.

2. Circle the whole arm (both arms at once) from the shoulder joint, making very small circles the size of a golf ball.

3. Breathe in for one circle, out for one circle.

REPEAT TEN TIMES, THEN DO TEN CIRCLES IN THE OPPOSITE DIRECTION.

EXERCISE 16
Side Reaches

Aim: to stretch the side of the torso safely, working the waist and lengthening the spine.

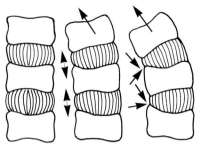

Lengthen up to keep the gap.

Without lengthening first you risk squashing the discs.

Lengthening the side of the body is very important. Our everyday movements simply don't give us the stretching out exercises that the body needs. Not only does this feel terrific, it is vital to the health of the back. Tightness in the Quadratus Lumborum muscle, which is one of the muscles this exercise works, can contribute to an overly hollow back.

Warning: If you have a severe back problem, especially a disc-related problem, do not attempt do this exercise.

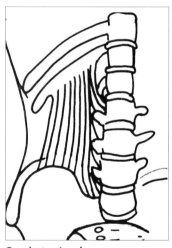

Quadratus Lumborum

Remember to keep lengthening upwards with the spine. If you simply bend to the side you may 'squash' the vertebrae together. By lengthening the spine first, you increase the gaps between the vertebra and prevent them from grating on each other. The same principle applies to twisting with the spine: remember to lengthen up first.

Watchpoints:
✔ Keep both buttocks firmly anchored to the seat of the chair.
✔ Lengthen up through the spine, lifting out of the hips, reaching up towards where the ceiling meets the wall.
✔ Keep your head and neck in line with the spine. Don't be tempted to look down.
✔ Be careful not to arch the lower back.
✔ Remember 'navel to spine' (see page 40).

EQUIPMENT
■ A sturdy chair (not too wide)

STARTING POSITION
Sit astride a turned-around chair –
if this is uncomfortable, sit in the
normal fashion.

★ACTION
1. Place one hand on the
back of the chair in front
of you.

2. Raise the other hand
over your head, with the
palm facing downward.

3. Breathe in and then
lengthen up through the
spine.

4. Breathe out, navel to
spine, as you reach across
to the top corner of the
room lifting out of your
hips and through the
waist, keeping your
bottom firmly planted on
the chair, keeping your
hips square. Lengthen
slowly, then release. Do
this three times,
breathing out as you
stretch, and breathing in
as you release.

5. Breathe in as you return to
centre.

6. Breathe out as you lower the
arm, opening wide, as in 'The
Corkscrew' (see page 56).

**REPEAT THREE TIMES TO EACH
SIDE.**

EXERCISE 17
Waist Twist

Warning: Take care if you have a back problem.

Aim: to work the waist, while achieving the correct positioning of the upper body without creating tension. And to work between the shoulder blades, opening out the front of the shoulders.

This is a deeper, complementary stretch to the 'Hip Rolls' that you did in the warm-up (Exercise 13, page 54). There, you stabilized the upper body as you twisted the lower half. Here it is the lower part of the body that is stabilized.

Think of yourself as pivoting around a fireman's pole, i.e. around your spine.

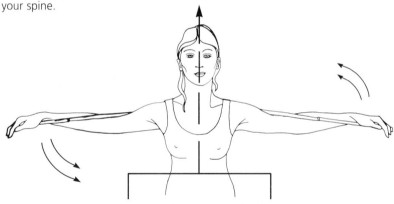

Keep pelvis square and still.

Watchpoints:
✔ Keep your hips square. If you don't, you'll miss the stretch.
✔ Don't lean forwards or backwards. Keep lengthening up, up, up.
✔ Don't let the back arch; remember 'North to South' (page 20) with a neutral spine.
✔ Don't 'lead' with one shoulder.

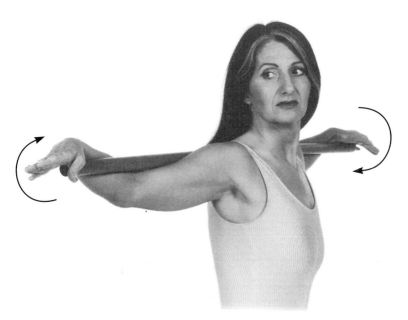

EQUIPMENT
■ A pole about 1.5 to 1.8 metres (five to six feet) in length – a strong, thick bamboo cane is ideal as it retains some flexibility
■ A chair (optional)

STARTING POSITION
This exercise can be done either on the chair or standing. It is probably better to begin by sitting until you can learn to keep the pelvis square while twisting the body.

  Place the pole across your shoulders, taking your arms around and under with hands resting on the pole. If this is too uncomfortable, hold your arms out to the side. When they tire, lower them as necessary.

★ACTION
1. Breathe in as you lengthen up through the spine.

2. Breathe out, 'navel to spine' and, keeping your pelvis square and facing forward, gently twist your body around as far as is comfortable. Your head will also turn. Only turn as far as you can, while keeping your pelvis square and still.

REPEAT UP TO TEN TIMES ON EACH SIDE.

EXERCISE 18
Pole Raises

Aim: to learn to relax the shoulders while raising the arms, keeping tension out of the upper shoulder area. Open the chest, stretching the Anterior Deltoids. Learn the correct placement of the shoulder blades, working the Lower Trapezius muscle and the Latissimus Dorsi muscle.

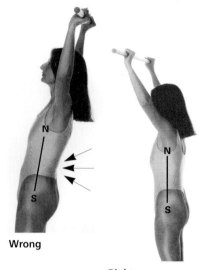

Wrong

Right

We have already seen how tension in the upper shoulder area can develop and the negative effects that this can have on posture. This is a wonderful exercise for opening out the front of the shoulders, so countering round shoulders, and for developing the Lower Trapezius and the Latissimus Dorsi.

As above, don't allow the back to arch – maintain 'North to South' neutral spine alignment (see page 20).

Try not to duck your head as the pole comes over the top of it.

Aim to keep both shoulders and arms moving together, don't allow one shoulder to dominate. Keep reminding yourself of the 'Standing Instructions' (see page 31), lengthening the spine upwards.

Back view

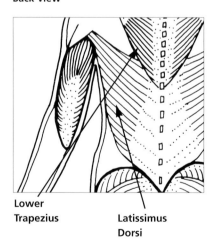

**Lower
Trapezius**   **Latissimus
                     Dorsi**

As you raise your arms, think of dropping the upper shoulders down.

Watchpoint:
✔ It is very important that you do not arch the back as you raise the arms – this often happens in order to compensate for any lack of rotation in the shoulder joint.

EQUIPMENT
■ Any pole

STARTING POSITION
Stand correctly, lengthening up through the spine. Hold the pole lightly, with both hands about a metre apart.

★ACTION
1. Breathe in as you raise the pole, allowing the movement of the hands and the pole to lead the arms and shoulders. Try to keep the upper shoulders relaxed, don't let them hike up around your ears. Think of them dropping down as the arms raise. Make the movement initiate from your shoulder blades.

2. Breathe out as you then bring the pole directly down behind you, keeping it close to your body and bending the elbows, so that you have a chicken-wing shape. Think of the ribs and the lower shoulder blades drawing down and together.

3. Breathe in as you slowly raise the pole from behind and breathe out as you bring the pole back down in front slowly.

REPEAT UP TO TEN TIMES.

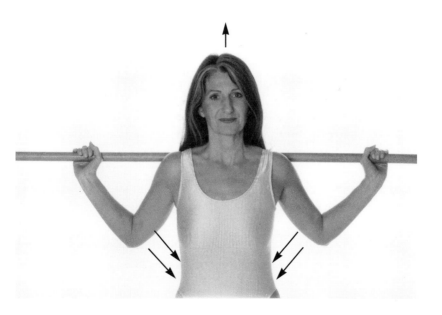

EXERCISE 19
Wrists, Hands & Fingers

Aim: to increase the flexibility in the hands and fingers and to work the wrist flexors and extensors.

Typing all day? Driving all day? These are just two of the thousands of activities we do which involve holding the arms and hands in an unnatural position. Repetitive strain injury (RSI) is caused by the same activity repeated over and over. You may have discovered when you completed your questionnaire that you do just that. It takes just a few minutes to help undo the damage, restoring the balance in the muscles.

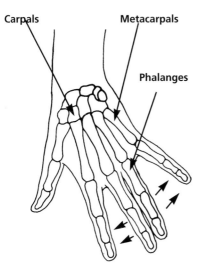

Carpals   Metacarpals

Phalanges

The bones of the hand.

At the other extreme, sometimes it isn't a repeated action but rather no action at all that causes the problem! Maintaining the flexibility of the fingers joints is very important,

keeping the joints open, mobile and well oiled. Only movement can do that!

Watchpoint:
✔ Don't tense the shoulders while working the arms and hands. Keep them relaxed and down.

STARTING POSITION
Stand correctly – you could also sit.

★ACTION 1
1. Breathe in to prepare, lengthening up through the spine.

2. With both elbows bent, breathe out as you extend both arms, flexing the hands back towards you, pushing through the wrist, the heel of the hand, the palms and the fingers. The action is as though you are pushing through water.

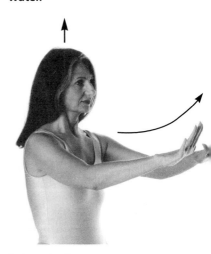

3. Breathe in as you recover.

REPEAT EIGHT TIMES.

★ACTION 2

1. Hold your hands out in front of you, keeping the elbows soft.

2. Take the first and second fingers together away from the fourth and fifth fingers, creating a gap in the middle.

3. Return to centre.

REPEAT EIGHT TIMES.

★ACTION 3

1. Leaving the second and third fingers in the centre, take the first and fifth finger away.

2. Return to centre.

REPEAT EIGHT TIMES.

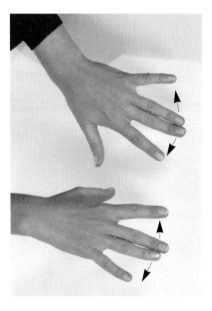

★ACTION 4

1. Play an imaginary piano, keeping the palms down.

2. Play an imaginary piano, with the palms up.

EXERCISE 20
Curl-ups

Aim: to strengthen the abdominals, especially the Rectus Abdominis muscle. Learn how to curl the upper body while keeping the navel pulled back to the spine and to use the spine as a wheel.

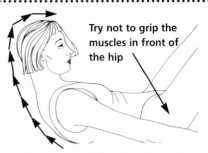

Curl the spine off the floor like a wheel

We have already discussed how a set of weak abdominals can contribute to back problems (see page 23). Curl-ups are a highly effective way of strengthening them.

For a curl-up to be efficient, the lower abdomen must stay hollowed out throughout the exercise.

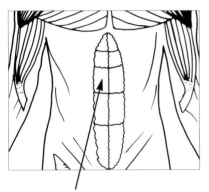

Rectus Abdominis

We have also asked you to maintain length in the front of your body. This is difficult to achieve, but an important aspect of the exercise. Without it, you are simply scrunching up the front of the body.

Curl-ups are so named because that is what you must do – curl up, not sit up. Carried out sloppily these are a waste of time, so take the time and do them slowly and carefully.

Once again, the image of a wheel is helpful.

If you think of curling your head and neck off the floor, it will help to release tension in the neck rather than creating it. Think of softening the breastbone as you curl up. It will help you to curl.

Don't forget to open out the elbows when you have completed each curl-up. It will help to discourage round shoulders.

Warning: If you have any neck problems, such as whiplash, it is better to leave this exercise out. There are plenty of alternatives, shown later in the book, which work the abdominals – for example, the 'Single Leg Stretch' (Exercise 23, page 74) with a pillow to support the upper body, or Stage 1 of 'The Star' (Exercise 27, page 88).

Do not proceed with the exercise if it feels uncomfortable.

Watchpoints:
✔Keep the lower abdominals hollowed out as you come up.
✔ Keep squeezing the inner thighs together.
✔ Keep the back of your neck long and the shoulders relaxed, but do not tuck the chin in too far. Keep a gap there.
✔ Don't lift your tailbone up off the floor. Keep it lengthening away from you and try not to tighten up around your hip joints.

EQUIPMENT
■ Tennis ball
■ Small, flat pillow

STARTING POSITION
Lie on your back with your feet together, flat on the floor and knees bent and pressing together. Place the tennis ball between the knees and put the pillow underneath your head. Squeeze the buttocks.

As an alternative position, you may have your feet on a wall with the knees at an angle of ninety degrees, so that the back remains flat on the floor.

★ACTION
1. Begin by placing one hand on the side of your head. Place the other hand on your lower abdominal muscles. You keep squeezing the inner thighs together throughout the exercise.

2. Breathe in to prepare.

3. As you start to breathe out, hollow out the lower abdominals, dropping them back to the spine, lengthening the base of the spine. The tailbone stays down and lengthens away from you.

4. Maintaining the length in the front of the body, slowly lift your head to look at your stomach, gently curling the neck and shoulders, if possible, off the floor. Keep the back of the neck long, but do not tuck the chin in.

5. Only go so far as you can keep your stomach hollowed out. The minute your stomach begins to pop up, curl back down. It is imperative that you do not pull on the neck!

6. Breathe in as you slowly curl back down.

7. Open the elbow right back to the floor each time you go down.

REPEAT FIVE TIMES, THEN CHANGE HANDS AND DO FIVE MORE.

Curl-ups –
THE ADVANCED VERSION
When you have mastered keeping the stomach hollowed out, you may place both hands by the side of your ears.
   Open both elbows out and down at the end of each curl-up.

EXERCISE 21
Oblique Curl-ups

Aim: to work the oblique stomach muscles without stressing the neck and maintaining the curling action of the spine.

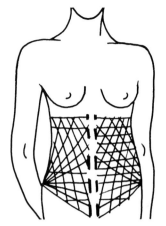

The obliques criss-cross the torso like a corset.

As the name suggests, you are now working on the oblique stomach muscles which criss-cross the abdomen and are active in flexing, twisting your trunk and bending it to the side. These muscles are sorely underused and yet they are very important to maintaining postural fitness. When you bring your left elbow towards your right knee, you are working the left oblique external, the right oblique internal and the rectus abdominis! When you bring your right elbow towards your left knee, you are working the right oblique external and the left oblique internal. Either way, it's hard work!

EQUIPMENT
- Tennis ball
- Small, flat pillow

Warning: Do not attempt this exercise if you have any neck problems.

Watchpoints:
✔ Do not jerk – keep the movement smooth.
✔ Check your neck – watch it doesn't strain.
✔ Keep squeezing the inner thighs together, but keep your tailbone down and the muscles around the hip joints relaxed.
✔ Keep the lower abdominals hollow!

STARTING POSITION
Begin as for 'Curl-ups' (Exercise 20), page 68. Place a tennis ball between the knees and put a pillow under the head.

★ACTION
1. Place both hands at the side of your ears. You will keep squeezing the inner thighs together throughout the exercise.

2. Breathe in to prepare, then, breathing out pull the navel to the spine hollowing, and gently and slowly curl up to take the left shoulder across towards the right knee, with the elbow staying open. Curl, do not jerk, keeping the back of neck long, but without tucking the chin in. The stomach stays hollow!

3. The base of the spine is then lengthened out and the tailbone stays down.

4. Breathe in, as you slowly curl back down.

5. Open elbows out and down to the floor.

REPEAT, ALTERNATING FIVE TIMES TO EACH SIDE.

★ACTION –
THE ADVANCED VERSION
1. Hold your hands together out in front of you, clasping them together.

2. Breathe out, navel to spine, and lift your head to look at your stomach. Then, imagining that someone is pulling your hands on a piece of string, move them to the left and lengthen away three times.

3. Breathe in as you come back through the centre of the body.

4. Breathe out and go over to the other side.

5. Lengthen three times. Breathe in as you come back to the centre and out as you come down again.

6. Repeat, coming back up to the side that you have just finished working on.

REPEAT TEN TIMES TO EACH SIDE.

EXERCISE 22

Turning Out the Leg

Aim: to learn to turn the leg out from the hip joint, without causing stress on the knees or ankles. To work the deep outward rotators of the leg.

Properly executed, the turnout has much to offer as it increases stability and strength, giving you a sense of widening from the centre. The range of motion of the legs is greatly increased because the Greater Trochanter, head of the thigh bone, is moved 'out of the way'. This offers the thigh bone much greater freedom of movement in its hip socket.

There are pitfalls, however, as dancers will testify. Incorrectly performed, the turnout is a disaster in the making, for, if you make the turnout from your knees or feet and force the movement, you will damage them both.

So how do you turn out safely? The answer lies in turning out the entire leg from the hip joint. The turnout is a movement that involves the rotation of the whole leg and not just the knee and below. The relationship or alignment of the knee, foot and ankle remains exactly the same as if the leg was facing forward in parallel.

Think of spiralling the leg out from the hip socket to the toes like a barber's pole.

You will be using the turnout in many of the Body Control exercises, such as the 'Single Leg Stretch' (Exercise 23, page 74).

Warning: If you have had any problems with sciatica, avoid turning out the leg. Simply work with the legs in parallel.

Watchpoints:
✔ Take care that the whole leg is turned out, not just the knees or feet.
✔ Ensure that the pelvis stays square.

STARTING POSITION
Stand in a balanced way.

★ACTION
1. Shift your weight onto your left leg.

2. Place your right hand onto your right hip joint.

3. Softly point the right foot and slide it away in front of you.

4. Rotate the whole leg outwards front hip, spiralling it out and around. You should feel the movement originate from the joint where your hand rests. The pelvis must stay square. Do not allow it to twist. Slide the leg back.

REPEAT THE MOVEMENT FIVE TIMES WITH EACH LEG.

EXERCISE 23
Single Leg Stretch

Aim: to strengthen the abdominal muscles and improve co-ordination and control. Learn to work the hip flexors and to use the inner thigh (Adductor) muscles to achieve maximum rotation in the hip joint (turnout).

A difficult exercise, but fabulous for strengthening the abdominals without straining the back and for achieving turnout. It requires great concentration and co-ordination – try planning your shopping or developing your Business Plan while doing this and see what happens!

You must read through all the instructions several times before attempting this exercise. Additionally, it would be a good idea to practise the hand movements on their own before continuing, as they take some mastering. Think about extending and spiralling the leg for miles – it has no end. Remember – lateral breathing is vital here, so breathe wide and full.

Try to keep the torso square, or, more appropriately, rectangular, i.e. don't let one side collapse downwards.

Warning: Always lower the head if the neck feels strained. If you have a neck problem or if you find the exercise too stressful for your neck, use a pillow or wedge to support the head and neck.

Watchpoints:
✔ When you first attempt this exercise, make sure that one knee is safely bent and held before the other one is extended. As you become more familiar with the movements, you can make both the hand exchange and leg stretch simultaneous.
✔ The movements must flow, and they need to be slow and controlled.
✔ At no time should there be any daylight under your back. Keep it firmly anchored to the floor. If you find that your back is arching, then raise the angle of the extended leg higher.

Keep hollowing

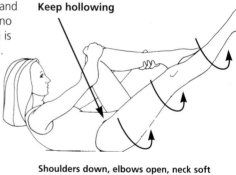

Shoulders down, elbows open, neck soft

✔ Check that your shoulders remain down and relaxed throughout the exercise.
✔ Your chin should be gently rotated towards your chest, but not tucked in, so that the back of the neck remains long.
✔ If you cannot reach your ankle, then hold the side of your shin.

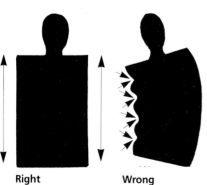

Right   **Wrong**

PLEASE READ THROUGH THE 'WATCHPOINTS' OPPOSITE VERY CAREFULLY, BEFORE ATTEMPTING THIS EXERCISE.

EQUIPMENT
■ If you have neck problems, you will need a large, firm pillow

STARTING POSITION
Lie on your back, draw your knees up onto your chest, one at a time with the toes just touching, but not the heels. Keep your feet softly pointed. Use a pillow if you have neck problems or if you feel your neck straining. Take hold of the outside of your calves. Your elbows are kept open to enable the chest to expand fully.

★ACTION
1. Breathe in as you soften the breastbone and slowly curl your head, neck and shoulders off the floor to look at your stomach – keep a gap under your chin, though. Leave your head on the pillow, if you are using one.

2. Breathe out and, anchoring navel to spine, stretch your left leg away, rotating the entire leg out from the hip joint so that it is at an angle of forty-five degrees to the floor. The toes are softly pointed.

3. Breathe in wide as you begin to bend the leg back onto your chest, bringing it back into your shoulder.

4. Change the hands so that now your left hand is on the outside of your left leg and your right hand is on the inside of your left knee. Breathe out, checking that the navel is still pulled back to the spine as you now extend the right leg, turning it out from the hip. Breathe in wide as the leg bends back into your shoulder.

REPEAT TEN TIMES WITH EACH LEG.

EXERCISE 24
The Hundred

Aim: to stimulate the circulation and breathing, this teaches control and how to stabilize the trunk and work without tension. To co-ordinate breathing with movement and improve stamina. Opening the upper back, working the abdominals and neck flexors correctly. To work the pectorals.

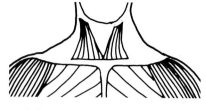

Neck flexors – use them but do not over-tense them.

The Hundred – there comes a time in each Body Control session when it is time to do the Hundred! Usually a groan echoes through the whole room! Yet everyone knows that they will feel tremendous afterwards, totally invigorated and refreshed.

We have given you a simplified version here and, yes, this is the simple version!

The importance of lateral/thoracic breathing, that is breathing into your sides or back, is clearly shown here. If you took your breath down into your lower abdomen, then your back would be left unprotected and may arch. Too shallow breathing will leave you short of oxygen. Refer back to Exercise 5, 'Breathing Correctly' (page 38) to remind you of lateral breathing.

The neck flexor muscles are key postural muscles. Usually the neck extensor muscles are powerful and tight. This exercise stretches them, while working the opposing neck flexors.

Warning: This is a difficult exercise and should not be attempted until you are confident that you can perform it without strain or stress. Read through the instructions several

times. Practise the beating and breathing before adding the raised legs. Please do not push yourself on too fast. If in doubt, leave it out!

Leave your head on the pillow if you have neck problems. If you have a back problem, consult your practitioner first.

Watchpoints:
✔ At no time should your back leave the floor – keep it anchored. If it feels as though it might arch, then bring your knees nearer to you. Don't let them fall away!
✔ Bring your head down onto the pillow, if you feel your neck straining.
✔ The beating action should not jar at all into the shoulders – keep the elbows very slightly bent.
✔ Keep the abdomen hollowed out.
✔ There are two stages to learning this exercise. Do not progress to the next stage until you are confident that you are ready.

STARTING POSITION – STAGE 1
Lie on your back. Bend your knees up onto your chest, one at a time and in parallel. Arms are extended alongside your body, palms down, wrists straight and head down.

★ACTION – STAGE 1
1. Breathing in wide into your sides and back, pump your arms up and down, no more than 15 centimetres (six inches) off the

floor for a count of five. The shoulder blades stay down with the arms lengthening away. Breathe out and pump the arms for a count of five.

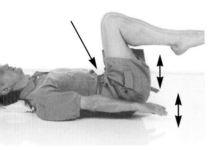

2. Continue to breathe in for five beats and out for five beats, until you reach up to 100. If you find the breathing too slow, reduce to three beats per breath.

3. When you have mastered co-ordinating the breathing with the arm movement, you can move on to the next part.

EQUIPMENT – STAGE 2
■ A pillow

STARTING POSITION – STAGE 2
1. Lie on your back. Bring your knees up onto your chest, one at a time, keeping the legs parallel. Straighten them up a little until you feel your abdominals working, but keeping the back down on the floor. Do not straighten the legs completely and do not let them fall away from you or your back will arch.

2. Have your feet flexed towards your face. Your arms are stretched along your body.

3. Palms are facing down with the wrists straight.

★ACTION – STAGE 2
1. Breathe in deeply to the sides of your body. As you breathe out, allow the lower abdominals to sink back towards the spine.

2. Slowly curl your head up so that you are looking down at your chest, but not tucking the chin too far in. You will need to soften your breastbone. The back of the neck stays long. Maintain a big gap between ears and shoulders.

3. Slowly pump your arms up and down 15 centimetres (six inches) above the floor, lightly tapping it. Shoulder blades stay down, arms length-ening along the floor and side of the body. Keep a large gap between ears and shoulders. Co-ordinate breathing with arm movements.

4. Breathe in for five beats. Breathe out for five beats. You are aiming to beat a total of 100 times, that is 20 x 5 beats.

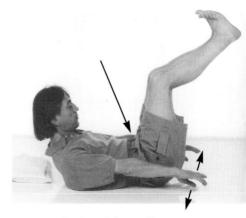

5. Bring the head down if your neck feels sore. Bend the knees down onto your chest when you have finished. Come down if neck feels strained.

EXERCISE 25
Curl-downs

Aim: to strengthen the deep abdominals, thus promoting endurance. Learn how to curl the spine, creating flexibility and strength.

Strong abdominals and a flexible spine, control and co-ordinated breathing: all these are achievable with practice and this exercise is superb in developing these attributes. It also has a wonderful 'feel good' factor as you begin to realize your potential.

This exercise strengthens the deep abdominals, enhancing the muscle control of each segment of the spine. It also increases the articulation of each vertebra of the spine via the wheeling movement. It is important with these exercises to use the muscles in the most efficient sequence, for it is this that aids the mobilization of the spine. It demands that you relax certain muscles, focusing on, and isolating others.

If you allow your abdomen to bulge then you are no longer using the right muscles. So, keep hollowing, hollowing, hollowing. Try to release the muscles around the hip joint.

Warning: This is a difficult exercise which requires strength. Consult your practitioner if you have a back problem. Stop at once if your back hurts.

Watchpoints:

✔ It is vital, however, that you perform this exercise with control. If you feel yourself coming down too fast or you feel any strain in your back, stop and wait a few weeks until you are stronger and more flexible.

✔ You will only put yourself back if you take on too much – listen to your body.

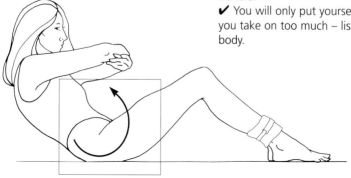

EQUIPMENT
■ A long scarf, or similar
■ A pillow

STARTING POSITION
Sit on the floor with your knees bent, feet flat on the floor and together. Wrap the scarf around the front of the legs just below the knees. Place leg weights around your ankles. Place a pillow under your head.

★ACTION
1. Holding onto the scarf, rotate your head forward so that your chin is in the direction of your chest, but a gap remains.

2. Breathe out and tilt the pelvis forward so that the pubic bone comes up to meet your chin, hollowing out your lower abdominals.

3. Holding onto the scarf, slowly curl the back right down onto the floor, one vertebra at a time.

4. Keep curling, curling, curling; keep hollowing, hollowing, hollowing. Try to release the muscles around your hips.

5. If your abdominals pop up, stop and try again when you are stronger. Repeat eight times.

6. Each time you have finished curling down, sit up again in a normal, comfortable way – you may use your elbows or roll onto your side. (Coming up isn't part of the exercise).

1

Curl-downs –
THE ADVANCED VERSION

When you feel confident, try the exercise without the scarf (see opposite). But you must be in control!

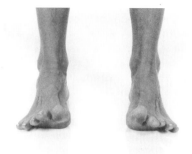

Pilates was a great discovery for me 10 years ago, and has become a way of life. In a full and sometimes stressful life it brings tranquillity and balance.

Pilates is a mind, body exercise that strengthens and tones my body without building muscle.

It promotes energy and vitality and enhances my emotional equilibrium.

LINDKA CIERACH

A Sound Foundation – Foot Control

The foot is a miracle, and movement is a hymn to the miracle.
MARTHA GRAHAM

How we neglect our feet! Each day, we try to squeeze them into shoes that are often too tight or with heels too high, and then forget about them until they start to protest and hurt; then we put them up (usually with the cup of tea), only to forget about them once again. Even trainers, which are generally 100 percent better than most shoes, still deny us that wonderful feeling you get from going barefoot.

When evolution 'designed' the foot, it expected us to be romping through fields, climbing over rocks and stony ground, gripping slippery surfaces. All this action would have given the feet a natural workout, keeping them strong and flexible.

Every reflexology point on the base of the feet would have been naturally massaged by the ground, so stimulating the rest of the body.

What do we have to offer our feet today? Fourteen-plus hours cramped in the same shoes, walking on flat, even pavements. It is no substitute. Even when taking part in sport, we often forget the feet. Once we've chosen the right training shoes for the sport, we assume that's enough, but can you imagine putting your hands in a shoe-like glove and then ignoring them all day?

But look at what the feet do for us! They are our contact point with the earth. They bear the entire weight of our bodies and they really are the foundations upon which our bodies are built. And like most foundations, they need to be stable, to be able to bear our weight in a balanced way. Muscles remember long-accustomed habits, regardless of whether they are good or bad. If we can get our feet right, then the knees, upper legs, hips, pelvis and more will all be in far better alignment.

If you allow the feet to roll in (pronation) or roll out (supination), you have then upset the balance and your posture will be affected. You can easily tell if you are prone to rolling in or out by checking your shoes. See if they have worn more on the outside or the inside of the heel. Similarly, you can easily spot if you put your weight more on the front or the back of your foot, as the toes of the shoes will curl up or the heels will be worn down in excess.

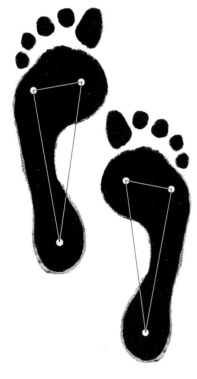

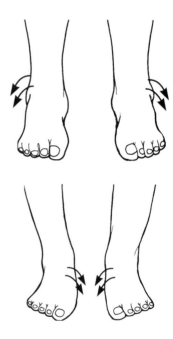

When we give you instructions for standing correctly, we start with the feet. Mentally draw a triangle on each foot, from the base of the big toe to the base of the smallest toe to the centre of the heel. You need to ground yourself on those two triangles with the weight evenly centred on them.

The exercises on the following pages are just a few ways through which you can help to realign and reawaken the feet.

By the way, all these foot exercises are great to do in an aeroplane or on any other long journey, as they can help prevent swollen ankles and will stimulate the circulation in the feet.

EXERCISE 26A
Foot Circling

Aim: to achieve maximum rotation in the ankle joint.

Mobility in the ankle joint is the goal of this exercise. For most of us, the foot only really hinges on the ankle as we go about our everyday activities. Rarely do the feet get the opportunity to rotate in this fashion, so your body will literally scream 'thank you' as you do these foot circles!

EQUIPMENT
■ A rolled-up towel or pillow, if necessary

STARTING POSITION
Sit on the floor with your legs extended in front of you, a little more than a hip-width apart. Your knees should be facing directly up to the ceiling.

If you are uncomfortable in this position, roll up a towel or pillow and place it under your buttocks to tilt you forward slightly. You can place your hands on the floor beside you to stabilize you.

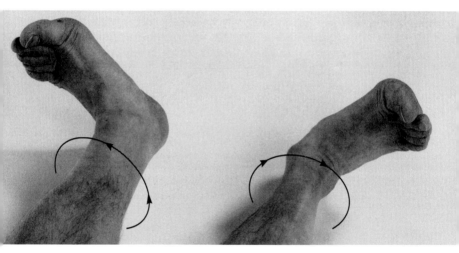

Watchpoints:
✔Keep the knees still and in good alignment with your hips.
✔Circle the feet very slowly – notice how the muscles in your legs are working.

★ACTION
1. Lift up out of the hips, with your spine straight, 'navel to spine' (see page 40).

2. Rotate the feet around in circles in an outward direction. Keep the knees still and work from the ankles – don't just twiddle your toes around!

REPEAT TEN TIMES IN EACH DIRECTION.

EXERCISE 26B
Lifting the Arches

Aim: to strengthen the arches of the foot, preventing flat feet.

Flat feet can change your whole postural stance, shortening the Achilles' tendon and causing both upper and lower back imbalance. If the arches are weak, it will also contribute to the habit of rolling in the inside of the foot, again upsetting the foundations on which good posture are built. The arches are the shock absorbers of the feet – they literally put the spring in our step!

Transverse arch   **Longitudinal arch**

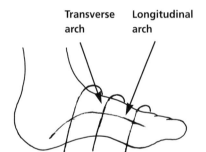

The arches of the foot.

EQUIPMENT
■ A rolled-up towel or pillow, if necessary

STARTING POSITION
Sit on the floor with your knees bent, feet flat on the floor and in parallel. Alternatively, you can simply stand correctly or sit on a chair, with your feet on the floor, whichever is the most comfortable.

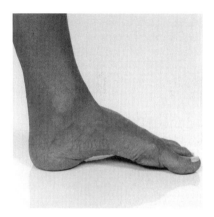

★ACTION
1. Keeping the toes long and not letting them scrunch up, lift the inner borders of your feet, increasing the arches, drawing the bones at the base of the toes back towards the heel.

2. Hold for fifteen seconds, and release.

REPEAT FIVE TIMES.

EXERCISE 26C

Pointing and Flexing

Aim: to learn how to point and flex the feet, while still maintaining good alignment in the rest of the legs. Learn to work and stretch the flexors and extensors of the foot.

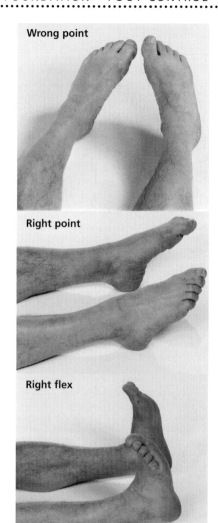

Wrong point

Right point

Right flex

To simplify the exercises, we refer to either pointing or flexing the feet. Different exercises require you to either point or flex, depending on which muscles we want you to work. But exactly what do we mean by pointing and flexing?

POINTING
By pointing the foot or toes, we intend that you should softly point them away from your face. A very common mistake is that you over-point and the foot then becomes 'sickled' (like a sickle). Instead, we want you to keep the front of the foot long and to make sure that the toes do not curl.

FLEXING
By flexing the foot, we intend that you push your heel away from your face. The toes will come up towards your face but again, they should not curl over. Keep them long, with the heel lengthening away.

Point

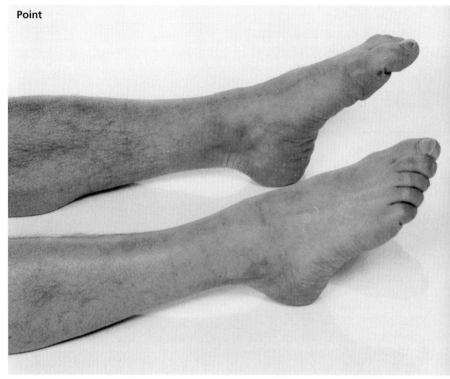

STARTING POSITION
As for Exercise 26a, but bring the legs in a little so that they are a hip-width apart.

★ACTION
Keep lifting out of your hips, do not slouch. Alternately, point and flex the foot, keeping the knees in line with the hips.

Flex

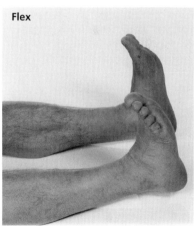

EXERCISE 26D

Waking Up the Toes – The Mexican Wave!

Aim: to work the toes individually, reawakening them.

Control your body! That includes the toes – all of them! Believe us, this is a very difficult exercise and one which may take you a lifetime to perfect! Just remember that any progress, however gradual, is tremendous. If you do succeed, it makes a great after-dinner party trick!

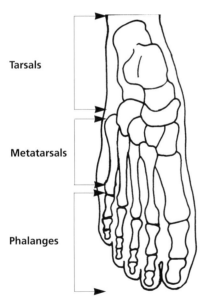

Tarsals

Metatarsals

Phalanges

The bones of the foot.

Watchpoints:
✔Keep the bones at the base of your toes (the metatarsals) flat on the floor.
✔Don't let the heel come off the floor.
✔Don't let the feet roll.

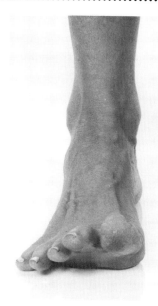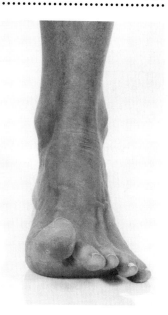

STARTING POSITION
As for Exercise 26c.

★ACTION
1. Separate your toes, lifting them off the floor one at a time like a Mexican wave.

2. Place them back on the floor one by one, beginning with the little toe and keeping them as widely spaced out as possible.

3. You may need to use your hands to help to isolate the toes and to move each of them individually!

REPEAT FIVE TIMES WITH EACH FOOT.

There are three things I trust; The Lord, my family and Gordon's Body Control! Body Control leaves me confident in my physical appearance, alert and mentally confident and is the best therapy I know for aches and pains and for lifting your spirits. As for my body, just look at it, it has Gordon's handiwork (or is that footwork) stamped all over it! Body Control has been my only exercise system over the last twelve years and I cannot imagine being without it.

PATTI BOULAYE

Flexibility & Strength

EXERCISE 27
The Star

Aim: to locate and strengthen the abdominals, especially the Tranversus Abdominis muscle, right down to the pubic bone. Learn to lengthen and strengthen the back muscles. To work the deep outward rotators of the leg.

A very important exercise in the programme as it enables you to strengthen the back muscles without 'over-shortening' them. This exercise begins with you locating the lower abdominals and lifting them. In so doing, you are concentrating on the deepest layers of the stomach muscles, especially the Tranversus muscle. This is the muscle which holds the internal organs in place and helps to force air out of the lungs when you exhale.

Note: Don't lift the upper part of your abdominal muscles or you will allow the more superficial ones to take over. Think low, deep and corset-like!

With the second and third stages to the exercise, you are working on the major muscles of the back.

Watchpoints: Stage 1
✔ With the first part of the exercise, keep your back like a table-top. Don't move the lower back as you lift the stomach.
✔ Keep the elbows soft.

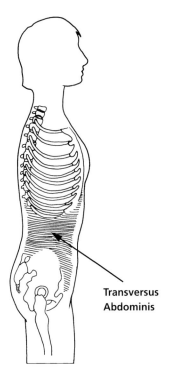

Transversus
Abdominis

STARTING POSITION – STAGE 1
Kneel on all fours. Your arms
should be directly beneath your
shoulders and apart, with your
knees beneath your hips and
apart. Your feet should be
lengthened out. Maintain the
natural neutral position of your
pelvis.

★ACTION – STAGE 1
1. Breathe in to prepare,
lengthening from the top of your
head to your tailbone.

2. Breathe out as you identify and
lift your lower abdominals from
your navel to your pubic bone, up
and back towards the spine. Your
back itself remains still.

REPEAT EIGHT TIMES.

STARTING POSITION – STAGE 2
Lie on your front. Rest your head on your folded hands, opening the shoulders out and relaxing the upper back. Your legs are shoulder-width apart and turned out with your feet long.

Back sufferers: You may need a small, flat pillow under your abdomen if your lower back is uncomfortable. If you have had sciatica, work with the legs in parallel.

★ACTION – STAGE 2
1. Breathe in to prepare, and then breathe out and lift the lower abdominals off the floor. Imagine that there is an egg beneath you that must not be crushed.

2. Still breathing out, lengthen the leg before you lift it NO MORE THAN 5 CENTIMETRES (two inches) off the floor, lengthening it away from the hip socket, keeping the leg straight, the foot long and the pelvis square on the ground.

3. Breathe in and relax it down.

REPEAT THREE TIMES WITH EACH LEG.

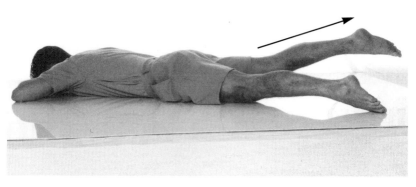

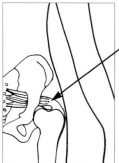

The piriformis muscle is one of the six deep outward rotators of the leg

Watchpoints: Stage 2 only
✔Take care to use only the muscles from the lower body. The upper back stays completely relaxed. Your head remains heavy on your hands. Think of creating space around the hip joint as you lengthen the leg away.

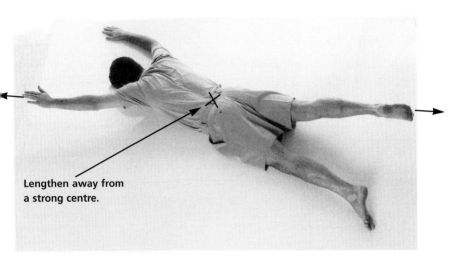

Lengthen away from
a strong centre.

STARTING POSITION – STAGE 3
As for stage 2, but take your arms
out so that you look like a star.
Place a small, very flat pillow
underneath your forehead.

★ACTION – STAGE 3
1. Breathe in to prepare and then
breathe out and lift – 'navel to
spine' (page 40).

2. Lift opposite arm and leg no
more than 5 centimetres (two
inches) off the ground,
lengthening but keeping the
centre strong. Don't twist in the
pelvis, both hip joints stay on the
floor.

3. Breathe in and relax. Repeat
with opposite side.

REPEAT FIVE TIMES EACH SIDE.

Watchpoints: Stages 2 and 3
✔Be careful to keep both hip joints
on the floor – you are only lifting the
leg.
✔Don't let the pelvis roll or twist –
keep it square.
✔Keep your neck long and relaxed,
the head stays down on the floor
throughout the exercise.
✔Everyone lifts the legs too high, so
aim to lift them just an inch or two.

EXERCISE 28
Single Heel-kicks

Aim: to lengthen the front of the thigh muscles (quadriceps) and to strengthen the hamstrings. Improve awareness and control of an action taking place out of sight behind you. To work the knee joint. In the sphinx position, to work the Erector Spinae, the back extensors (see exercise 29).

The 'Hamstring Stretch' (Exercise 8, page 44) stretches the hamstrings, but is equally important in strengthening them. As the hamstrings contract to bend the knee, the quadriceps must release to allow the movement. The releasing of the thigh muscles will eventually allow the full flexion (bending) of the knee joint, without stress on the joint itself.

The sphinx position involves the extension of the back. It is frequently recommended as a remedial exercise to back pain sufferers; however, some people find that this position is uncomfortable, pinching the lower back. If you find this to be the case, simply keep your head on the floor, until you have achieved greater flexibility in the lumbar region.

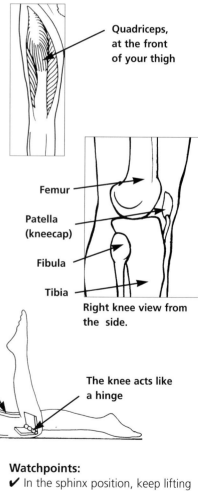

Quadriceps, at the front of your thigh

Femur

Patella (kneecap)

Fibula

Tibia

Right knee view from the side.

This exercise works on many levels.

Uses the back extensors

Strengthens the hamstrings

The knee acts like a hinge

Uses abdominals

Stretches the quadriceps

Watchpoints:
✔ In the sphinx position, keep lifting the navel to the spine.
✔ Make sure you keep the neck lengthening out from the shoulders.
✔ Keep the pelvis level.

STARTING POSITION
This exercise can be carried out either in a sphinx position or with the head down, resting on folded hands.

If you are coming up into the sphinx position, place the hands on the floor just wider than a shoulder-width apart. Drawing the navel back to the spine, gently push down onto the forearm to raise the upper body off the floor. The elbows stay down. Make sure that your neck remains long, the breastbone (sternum) stays in front, with the shoulders down. Your pelvis and pubic bone remain on the floor, the navel lifted to the spine throughout the exercise. You should feel comfortable in this position – if you feel any pinching in your back, come down to the alternative position. In the alternative position, rest your forehead on your folded hands. Make sure that your upper back remains open and relaxed at all times.

★ACTION
1. With the legs slightly apart, lift the navel to the spine and kick the right foot into the buttocks, keeping the foot pointed. Release the leg slightly, then flex the foot and kick again.

2. Repeat with the other foot.

3. Breathe in as one foot comes in, breathe out as the other foot comes in.

REPEAT FIVE TIMES WITH EACH FOOT.

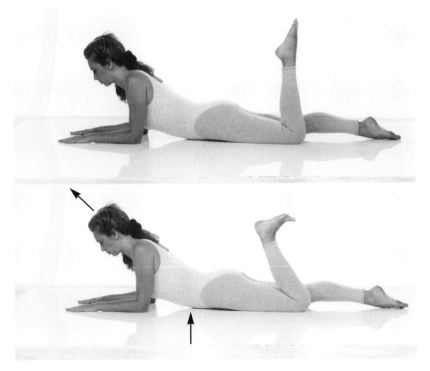

EXERCISE 29
The Cat

Aim: to achieve complete fluidity and control of the movement of the spine. Increase the flexibility of the spine and the awareness of the opening out of each vertebra.

A flexible, mobile spine, capable of moving fluidly and smoothly! Just watch a cat arch its back! This is nature at its very best.

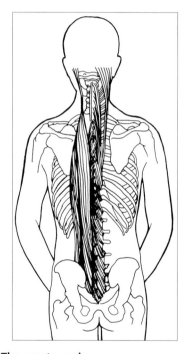

The erector spinae

The deep muscles of the back stabilise the vertebrae. They act like guy ropes on the spine and comprise many layers.

Watchpoints:
✔Don't lock into the elbows.
✔Don't lift the head – keep the back of the neck long and parallel to the floor.
✔Don't dip the back, just keep it in a parallel position.

STARTING POSITION
Kneel on all fours, your hands a little wider than a shoulder-width apart, placed directly beneath your shoulders, the fingers facing forwards. Your knees should be in line with your hips, with the toes stretched out.

You should look like a table, but with your spine maintaining its natural curve. This position itself is a wonderful exercise when you lengthen head to tailbone.

★ACTION
1. Breathe in to prepare.

2. As you draw the lower abdominals back and up towards the spine, breathe out then arch the spine up, opening it, wide, chin to chest, keeping the head and neck relaxed.

3. Next, breathe in.

4. Breathe out. Bring your head back up to parallel and your spine also to parallel. Lengthen your head away from your tailbone – the top of your head is being stretched away from your tailbone.

REPEAT EIGHT TIMES.

EXERCISE 30

Rest Position and Back-breathing

Aim: to lengthen and stretch out your sacral, lumbar, middle and upper spine. Learn control of your breathing in a relaxed position, to sense the filling and emptying of the lungs. To make maximum use of the lungs, taking the breath into the back.

This is a wonderful position in which to relax. It allows the spine to lengthen and refreshes the whole body. We have combined it here with back-breathing, as it is a perfect position to feel the movement in the back as the breath enters the lungs. Encourage that expansion.

Watchpoints:
✔ If you are uncomfortable in this position, use pillows as a support underneath your head, knees or buttocks, as appropriate, to help you to attain a comfortable position.
✔ Be careful to sit on your feet, not between them.

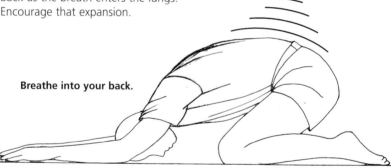

Breathe into your back.

Warning: If you have a knee injury, it may stress the joint so leave out the rest position. You can practise back-breathing while curled up on your side.

STARTING POSITION

If you have just done the 'Cat' (Exercise 29), you will be on all fours, your knees hip-width apart and directly under your hips, your hands just wider than your shoulders.

Now bring your feet together so that the toes are touching, the feet stretched long.

★ACTION

1. Breathe in to prepare.

2. Breathe out and slowly move back towards your buttocks. Do not raise your head or hands. Come back to sit on your feet – not between them – the back is rounded. Rest and relax into this position, leave the arms extended to give you a maximum stretch.

Back-breathing
STARTING POSITION

From the Rest Position, bring your hands round and place the heel of the hands on the lower ribs, with your fingers pointing toward your buttocks.

★ACTION

1. Breathe in deeply allowing the breath to fill the back of your lungs, moving your hands. You are breathing in to the count of 'five' and then breathe out to the same count of 'five'. You should feel the movement in your hands as your lungs expand and contract.

2. Take ten breaths.

3. When you have completed the exercise, gently unfold, bringing your head up last. Use the same method as for coming up after 'Roll-downs Against the Wall' (Exercise 2, page 32).

It was my theatrical agent who first whispered the name Gordon Thomson to me: some new method which lengthened muscles rather than beefing them up, which pulled in the stomach and lengthened the spine. [Gordon] took me and my body in hand. It literally changed day by day; there could be no mistake about it … I finally found my proper shape. There was no area of my life that didn't improve radically.

SIMON CALLOW

Working with Weights

The benefits of weight-bearing exercise

From birth until early adulthood, our muscles enlarge as we grow. Unfortunately, as we age and our lifestyle becomes less active, we lose muscle mass – in fact, some 20 to 40 percent by the time we reach the age of 80. The fibres shrink and are replaced by … you've guessed it … fat or connective tissue. And the central nervous system, which stimulates the fibres, finds it increasingly difficult to get the relevant message through and the muscle is less able to work without fatigue.

It seems, however, that many of these changes are linked as much to our sedentary lifestyle as to the ageing process itself … which means that if we work at it, we can prevent the muscles from becoming smaller and

The ordinary curves of the spine

The Dowager's Hump

weaker. With medical advances and improvements in nutrition, more of us can look forward to living longer, and it would be nice to think that we could still be active to be able to enjoy those remaining autumn years.

It isn't only the muscles that are

affected as we grow older. Fractures that are caused by osteoporosis, which is the thinning of bones, are a major risk for the elderly. One in three women in Britain will fracture their wrist, hip or spine, and one in five of these will die within a year of the accident. There are low-dose x-rays which can measure bone density. Visually, the earliest signs are often height loss and an increased curvature of the spine – the all-too familiar 'Dowager's Hump'.

That's the bad news. The good news is that more and more is being written on the value of weight-training for the prevention of osteoporosis in both menopausal and post-menopausal women. Recent research has shown that regular exercise, weight-training and a calcium-rich diet can together help prevent brittle bones.

To be beneficial, the exercise must be weight-bearing and, even then, only the sites targeted by that exercise will benefit because the bone loading effect is very specific, i.e. the leg weight exercises are not going to increase the bone density of your arms!

But will you end up with large, bulging muscles? Not if you follow the instructions carefully and stick to the size of weights we recommend. You will basically develop a healthier ratio of muscle to fat. You may put on a little weight as muscle weighs more than fat, but you'll certainly look leaner and firmer – and feel much better.

All of the exercises given can be done without weights at all. In fact, we recommend that you first attempt them without weights to perfect your technique and to slowly build up your muscle strength. When you are confident, then start to use home-made weights such as a 115g (4oz) can of beans or bag of rice, then 175g (6oz), 225g (8oz). Only invest in purchased weights when you are comfortable with the exercises.

Remember, we recommend that the arm weights weigh up to 900g (2lb) each (a 2.7kg/4lb pair), and the leg weights up to 1.1kg (2.5lb) each (a 2.7kg/5lb pair).

EXERCISE 31

Leg Weights – Abductor Lifts

Aim: this series of exercises is designed to strengthen the abductors (outer thigh), the gluteals (buttocks) and also the muscles of the sacral lumbar (lower back). It also tones the upper leg and controls cellulite.

A very popular exercise! You are working the abductor muscles which run along the outside of the thigh and buttocks.

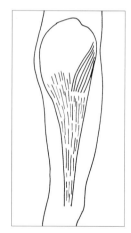

Side view

Tensor fasciae latae

With each of these exercises it is vital to 'stabilise' the torso using your deep abdominals (navel to spine). The ability to maintain 'core stability' while moving your limbs is one of our main objectives. **Only use weights when you feel comfortable with the exercise.**

Watchpoints:
✔ Keep the 'navel to spine' (page 40), so that you protect the lower back and prevent it from arching or the waist from dropping down to the floor.
✔ Lengthen the heel as far away as possible from the hip ... keep a long, long leg.
✔ Keep the rotation inward from the hip; be careful not to turn it in just from the ankle.
✔ Keep lifting the waist off the floor and lengthening the body.
✔ If you are lucky enough to lack any natural padding around your hips, you may find it uncomfortable to lie like this. If so, just put a small piece of foam underneath your hip.

This is the first exercise in a series of four which can be completed on one side, before you turn over to repeat the series on the other side of the body.

EQUIPMENT
Practise these exercises first without weights until you are totally familiar with them and they cause you no discomfort. You may then strap leg weights of up to 1.1 kg (2.5lb) onto your ankles. Start with the lightest weight.

STARTING POSITION
Lie on your right side in a straight line – this is crucial so, if you like, you can lie up against a wall to check your alignment. Don't lean on the wall! Remember 'North to South' alignment.

Your right arm is stretched out, your head resting against the arm. Bend your right leg in front of you – if viewed from above, you'll look like a letter 'h' shape on its side. This will give you a slight pelvic tilt to protect the lumbar spine.

Use your left arm to support yourself in front. Throughout the exercise, keep lifting the waist off the floor and maintain the length in the trunk.

★ACTION
1. Raise your left leg so that it is in line with your hip – about 12.5 centimetres (five inches) off the floor. Be careful not to take it behind you!

2. Rotate the leg in slightly from the hip and flex the foot towards your face.

3. Breathe out as you slowly lift the leg about 15 centimetres (six inches), then breathe in and lower. Raise and lower the leg ten times, without returning it to the floor. Breathe out as you raise and in as you lower.

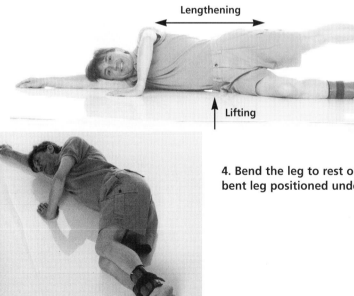

Lengthening

Lifting

4. Bend the leg to rest on the bent leg positioned underneath.

EXERCISE 32 & 33

Leg Weights – Lift and Lower and Leg Weights – Twenty Lifts

Aim: to work the abductor muscles (tensor fascia latae) and the gluteal muscles.

This is terrific for strengthening the muscles of the buttocks and lower back. The gluteals are important postural muscles. Weaknesses here can affect your whole alignment. You will be amazed at how difficult this exercise is when you first attempt it – this is especially true if your other leg muscles are over-developed.

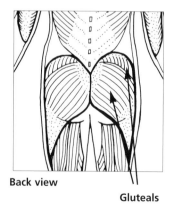

Back view

Gluteals

You may notice that you are working the underneath leg as well, as it stabilizes you!

Warning: These are advanced exercises. Do not attempt them until you are very comfortable with Exercise 31. Take medical advice if you have a back injury.

Watchpoints:
✔ Remember to keep the leg straight and gently rotated in from the hip throughout the exercise.
✔ The foot remains flexed.
✔ Make sure that your hip stays back, and the lower back straight in a 'North to South' alignment.
✔ Keep using the abdominals to support your back totally .
✔ As you bring the leg back in front of you, be careful that you don't take it behind you or your back will arch.
✔ Keep the length in the trunk, with the waist working to keep it from collapsing into the floor.
✔ Don't be tempted to use weights that are far too heavy.

EQUIPMENT
■ **Leg weights (if using)**

STARTING POSITION
As in 'Abductor Lifts' (Exercise 31).

★ACTION
1. Slowly raise your leg until it is 12 centimetres (five inches) off the floor and on a level with your hip joint. Rotate the whole leg in from the hip joint, flexing the foot, with your toes toward your face.

2. Breathe in to prepare and breathe out navel to spine as you bring your leg slowly out in front of you. You are aiming for an angle of ninety degrees with the back, but work up to this gradually.

3. Raise and lower the straight leg no more than 12 centimetres (six inches) in a line with your hips. Breathe in as you raise the leg, and out as you lower it.

4. Return the straight leg back to the starting position.

5. Repeat ten times, without lowering the leg to the floor. Breathe in as you raise the leg, and out as you lower it. Then bend the knee and relax the leg on the one underneath.

Twenty Lifts
(ADVANCED EXERCISE)

STARTING POSITION
As for Exercise 32.

★ACTION
1. From the starting position, raise the leg, rotate in from the hip joint, and flex the foot. Breathe in to prepare.

2. Breathe out navel to spine, and bring the leg in front to ninety degrees with the back.

3. Raise and lower the straight leg just 15 centimetres (six inches), at hip height, keep lengthening the body, lifting the waist.

4. Repeat up to twenty times, breathing in for five lifts and out for five lifts.

5. Note the change in the breathing pattern – now you are breathing out as you raise and in as you lower.

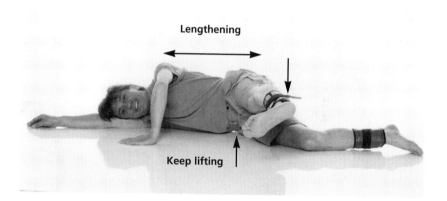

Lengthening

Keep lifting

Lengthening

EXERCISE 34
Leg Weights – Inner-thigh Toner

Aim: to tone up the inner adductor muscles. To achieve core stability.

It is quite surprising how weak these muscles become, especially when the other leg muscles are strong in comparison. You must always strive to keep a balance in strength between the different leg muscles.

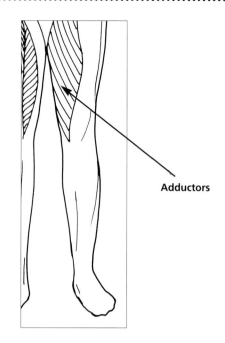

Adductors

Watchpoints:
✔ Keep working the abdominals, don't let the waist sag into the floor.
✔ Check that you are moving the whole leg together and not just twisting from the knee.
✔ Don't let your foot sickle (curl) round to help you come up further. The action must be in the inside of the thigh.

STARTING POSITION

Stay on your left side, but now bend your top knee and drop it in front of you. Do not let the hip roll forward, one hip bone stays directly above the other. If you feel you are rolling forward, you may rest your knee on a pillow. Stretch the bottom leg away, turning it out from the hip joint. Point the toe.

★ACTION

1. Breathe in to prepare.

2. Keeping the leg turned out from the hip, long and straight, breathe out as you lift navel to spine and slowly raise the underneath leg. Keep lengthening the leg away. Keep the length in your waist. Do not collapse.

3. Breathe in as you lower the leg.

REPEAT UP TO TWENTY TIMES.

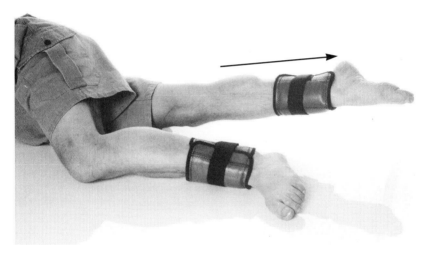

When you have completed Exercises 31–34, you can then turn over and do the complete leg weight series on other side, starting back at Exercise 31.

EXERCISE 35
Arm Weights – Flys

Aim: to open the chest and shoulders, and to tone the muscles of the arm. To strengthen the pectoral muscles.

The arm weight series of exercises (Exercises 35–38, pages 106–12) are designed to restore the correct balance in the upper body. They will strengthen the muscles around the shoulder and arm joints, but will not stress the joints themselves. They are also wonderful for opening the back.

Ideally, these exercises should be done on a bench, but it is also fine if they are performed on the floor.

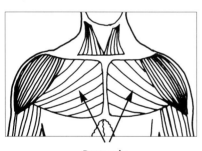

Pectorals

With the arm weight exercises, you will always do a series of ten and rest for 30 seconds before repeating the exercise – this is to allow the oxygen back into the affected muscles.

Warning: This exercise is not recommended if you have round shoulders, as it can reinforce the strength and tightness

Note that this is one of the few exercises where you breathe in as you initiate the movement. This is to help you expand the chest as you open the arms.

Watchpoints:
✔ Don't unfold the arms, i.e. don't hinge from the elbow – keep the natural curve.
✔ Take the arms directly to the side, rather than taking the weight behind you.
✔ Keep hollowing the abdominals – remember 'North to South' (page 20), neutral spine.
✔ Keep squeezing those inner thighs, but don't lift the tailbone – keep lengthening it away.

EQUIPMENT
■ Hand-held weights, of up to 1.1kg (2.5lb) per weight (to start with, it may be an idea to hold a 455g (1lb) bag of rice, then, when you feel this is easy, invest in hand-weights)
■ A bench, if you have one
■ Tennis ball

STARTING POSITION
Lie on your back, knees bent and together. Put the tennis ball between the knees. Keep your feet flat. Extend the arms, keeping the natural shape of the arm with the elbows slightly bent, as if you were hugging a large tree trunk.

★ACTION
1. Breathe in, as you open the arms directly to the side onto the floor, again keeping the natural shape. The elbows stay slightly bent.

2. Breathe out navel to spine, as you bring the arms back over your chest to be in line with your breastbone.

3. Keep squeezing the inner thighs together and hollowing out the lower abdominals.

REPEAT TEN TIMES.

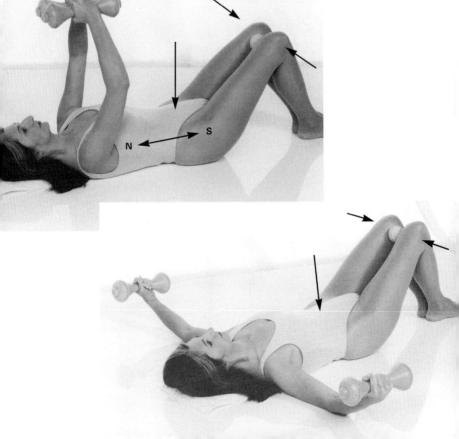

EXERCISE 36
Arm Weights – Backstroke Swimming

Aim: Learn to control the arms and open the shoulder blades. Combat round shoulders; work the shoulder joints and strengthen the deltoids, ligaments and tendons.

A wonderful exercise to counter those hunched positions we all find ourselves in every day. Enjoy the sensation of opening out ...

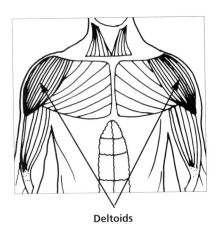

Deltoids

Watchpoints:
✔ As with the Exercise 35, don't arch the back, but remember 'North to South' (page 20)!
✔ As you take the arm behind you, keep it outside the line of the shoulder.
✔ If you are using a bench, keep the arm in line with the body and parallel to your side.
✔ Keep squeezing the inner thighs together, but don't lift the tailbone off the floor.

EQUIPMENT
■ Hand-held weights of between 455g and 900g (1 and 2lb) each
■ Tennis ball

STARTING POSITION
Lie on your back with your knees bent, a tennis ball placed between the knees. Keep your feet flat on the floor. Lie on a narrow bench, if possible. Holding the hand weights, raise your arms to the ceiling, keeping your palms away from your face with your elbows slightly bent.

★ACTION
1. Breathe in to prepare, breathe out navel to spine as you take the right arm behind you to the floor, and the left hand down to the side of your hip.

2. As you bring the arms back up to the starting position, breathe in.

3. Breathe out as you repeat the movement to the other side.

4. Keep squeezing the inner thighs and hollowing the lower abdominals.

REPEAT TEN TIMES TO EACH SIDE.

EXERCISE 37

Arm Weights – Triceps

Aim: to work the triceps only, with the rest of the body in total alignment and placement.

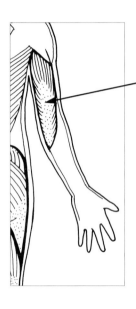

The triceps are at the back of your upper arms.

Watchpoints:
✔ Be careful not to arch the back. Remember 'North to South', neutral spine position (page 34).
✔ Don't close the arm in too much, keep a sense of width in the upper body and shoulders.
✔ Work solely between the hand and the elbow.
✔ Do not twist the wrist.
✔ Check that the neck is long, and that you are lengthening up through the spine.

EQUIPMENT
■ Hand-held weights of up to 1.1kg (2.5lb) each

STARTING POSITION
Sit on the floor with your knees bent in front of you and a tennis ball in between your knees. Alternatively, sit on a straight-backed chair, but without the ball. Hold the weight in your hand.

★ACTION
1. Lengthen up through the spine, lifting out of your hips.

2. Lift your arm, with the elbow bent to bring your hand behind your head.

3. Focusing on the shoulder and elbow, i.e. not moving them, raise the arm without locking into the elbow – about 30 centimetres (twelve inches) up, and then lower.

4. Breathe out as you raise the arm, breathe in to recover.

REPEAT TEN TIMES.

EXERCISE 38
Arm Weights – Biceps

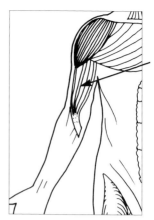

Biceps – at the front of your arms.

Aim: to work the biceps, controlling the arm movement without jerking and keeping the whole body stable.

This is a common exercise practised in gyms throughout the country. It is the way that you approach the exercise that is important, for the body must remain in good alignment and the action should not rock the body or it will jar into the spine. Use the second weight to help stabilize you.

Watchpoints:
✔ Keep the elbow isolated and still. If you find it keeps moving, put the other weight down and steady. Use the other hand to steady just inside the elbow.
✔ Keep reminding yourself of the correct standing instructions, lengthening up through the spine (see page 31).

EQUIPMENT
■ Hand-held weights of up to 1.1kg (2.5lb) each

STARTING POSITION
Stand correctly, with the feet slightly apart. Hold one weight in each hand. Keep your arms down by your side, with the palms forward on the arm you wish to exercise.

★ACTION
1. To prepare, breathe in, lengthening up through the spine.

2. Breathe out navel to spine and raise the arm, keeping the elbow quite still and close into your side. Your hand will finish close to your shoulder joint.

3. Breathe in as you return the arm to your side. Repeat ten times with one arm, and then switch to the other.

4. Work up towards doing a set of three on each side.

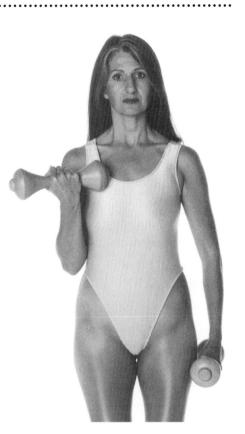

After my session with Gordon I felt that I'd learned a lot about the way my body works, and believe that the sports world has much to learn from Pilates exercises – if athletes paid more attention to flexibility, there might be fewer injuries.

SHARRON DAVIES

The Wind-down

The two exercises on the following pages are designed to help you to wind down following a session of exercises. Do not be tempted to skip them as they are very important. They will also help you to centre yourself and relax the joints, muscle ligaments and tendons, as well as your internal organs after exercising. The breathing will help you to achieve a sense of fulfilment after working intensely with your own body. Take a few moments to relax and register how you feel after the session.

It is a good idea to lie in the Relaxation Position (Exercise 4, page 36) for as long as you wish at the end of a workout.

EXERCISE 39
Arm Openings

Aim: to wind down the body by relaxing the upper body while opening the chest and to achieve a sense of 'openness' while centring.

Be completely aware of your arm and hand as it displaces the air moving through space.

Watchpoints:
✔ Make sure that your knees are really well curled up, and try to keep them together.
✔ Your head must follow your hand movement.
✔ Keep your elbows soft.
✔ Only 'open' as far as you are comfortable.

EQUIPMENT
■ **A pillow**

STARTING POSITION
Lie on your side, with your knees well curled up. Your back should be in a 'straight' line. You should have a pillow under your head. Your arms are extended in front of you, with your palms together at shoulder height.

★ACTION
1. Breathe in as you slowly extend and lift the upper arm, keeping the elbow soft, opening out like a door. Keep your eyes on your hands so that the head follows the arm movement. You are aiming to touch the floor behind you, but do not force it.

Try to keep your knees together and your navel to spine throughout.

2. Breathe out as you bring the arm back in an arc to rest on the other hand again. Repeat five times, then curl up on the other side and start again.

EXERCISE 40
Pillow Squeeze

Aim: to lengthen the spine and strengthen the stomach, the pelvic floor muscles and the adductors (inner thigh muscles). The action will also open your hip joints and widen the back.

This exercise will help to release stiff and tight muscles in the body. It helps to elongate the spine and to restore the internal organs to their proper place. Lifting the pelvic floor muscles can enhance your 'core stability', help prevent incontinence and prostate problems and improve your sex life!

Watchpoints:
✔ Don't let your neck join in the action – think of softening the breastbone and neck as you squeeze knees and inner thighs together.
✔ Keep your tailbone down and lengthening away. Remember 'North to South', neutral spine position page 20). Do not tuck under.
✔ Try to keep the muscles at the front of the hips relaxed.

EQUIPMENT
■ A large pillow

STARTING POSITION
Lie on your back, with your knees
bent. The feet are together and
placed flat on the floor. Keep arms
by your side. Open the knees and
place the folded pillow between
them.

★ACTION
1. Breathe in deeply to prepare.

2. Breathe out as you lengthen
the base of your spine, hollowing
the lower abdominals, lifting the
muscles of the pelvic floor (front,
back and middle passages) and
squeezing the inner thighs and
knees together. DO NOT TUCK
THE PELVIS. KEEP THE TAILBONE
ON THE FLOOR.

3. Now continue breathing
normally, while squeezing the
cushion for up to a count of ten,
then release.

REPEAT EIGHT TIMES.

Working Out with Body Control

Once you are familiar with the exercises, you will need to work out a schedule for practising them. Here are a few suggestions for combinations of exercises over the course of a week, depending on how long you wish the session to last:

✔ a short daily workout
✔ three sessions a week
✔ two sessions a week.

We have not given you an exact length of time for the workouts, because everyone works at different speeds.

If you fall into one of the common postural types given in the next chapter, 'The Correction of Common Postural Faults', you will need to include your remedial exercises as well.

A SHORT DAILY WORKOUT
You should include exercises from 'The Warm-up' section (pages 30-54) each time. You need not spend too long in the 'Relaxation Position' (page 36). We have not included any weight work (pages 98–112) in the short workouts, so you will need to add those in on the days when you have a little more time.

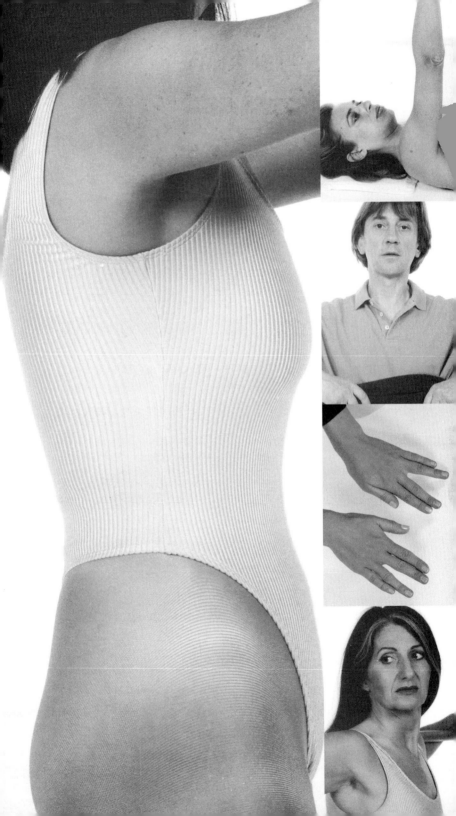

Day 1
Roll-downs Against the Wall –
  Exercise 2
Relaxation Position – Exercise 4
Breathing Correctly – Exercise 5
Navel to Spine – Exercise 6
Knee Circles & Leg Circles – Exercise 7
Hamstring Stretch – Exercise 8
Hip Flexors – Exercise 9
Shoulder Drops – Exercise 10
Neck Rolls & Nose Spirals – Exercise11
Spine Curls – Exercise 12
Hip Rolls – Exercise 13

Standing at Ease – Exercise 1
Side Reaches – Exercise 16

Curl-ups – Exercise 20
Oblique Curl-ups – Exercise 21

The Cat – Exercise 29
Rest Position – Exercise 30

Pillow Squeeze – Exercise 40

Day 2
Roll-Downs Against the Wall –
  Exercise 2
Relaxation Position – Exercise 4
Breathing Correctly – Exercise 5
Navel to Spine – Exercise 6
Knee Circles & Leg Circles – Exercise 7
Hamstring Stretch – Exercise 8
Hip Flexors – Exercise 9
Shoulder Drops – Exercise 10
Neck Rolls – Exercise 11
Spine Curls – Exercise 12
Hip Rolls – Exercise 13

Standing at Ease – Exercise 1

Waist Twist – Exercise 17
Single Leg Stretch – Exercise 23

Single Heel-kicks – Exercise 28
Rest Position & Back-breathing –
  Exercise 30
Arm Openings – Exercise 39

Day 3
Roll-downs Against the Wall –
  Exercise 2
Relaxation Position – Exercise 4
Breathing Correctly – Exercise 5
Navel to Spine – Exercise 6
Knee Circles & Leg Circles –
  Exercise 7
Hamstring Stretch – Exercise 8
Hip Flexors – Exercise 9
Shoulder Drops – Exercise 10
Nose Spirals – Exercise 11
Spine Curls – Exercise 12
Hip Rolls – Exercise 13

Standing at Ease – Exercise 1
The Corkscrew – Exercise 14
Wrists, Hands & Fingers – Exercise19

Curl-ups – Exercise 20
Oblique Curl-ups – Exercise 21

The Star – Exercise 27
Rest Position & Back-breathing –
  Exercise 30

Pillow Squeeze – Exercise 40

Day 4
Roll-downs Against the Wall –
  Exercise 2
Relaxation Position – Exercise 4
Breathing Correctly – Exercise 5
Navel to Spine – Exercise 6
Knee Circles & Leg Circles – Exercise 7
Hamstring Stretch – Exercise 8
Hip Flexors – Exercise 9
Shoulder Drops – Exercise 10
Neck Rolls – Exercise 11
Spine Curls – Exercise 12
Hip Rolls – Exercise 13

Standing at Ease – Exercise 1
Pole Raises – Exercise 18
The Samson – Exercise 15

Curl-downs – Exercise 25
  (if advanced otherwise Curl-ups –

Exercise 20)
Foot Control – Exercise 26

The Cat – Exercise 29
Rest Position – Exercise 30

Arm Openings – Exercise 39

Day 5
Roll-downs Against the Wall –
  Exercise 2
Sliding Down the Wall – Exercise 3
Relaxation Position – Exercise 4
Breathing Correctly – Exercise 5
Navel to Spine – Exercise 6
Knee Circles & Leg Circles – Exercise 7
Hamstring Stretch – Exercise 8
Hip Flexors – Exercise 9
Shoulder Drops – Exercise 10
Nose Spirals – Exercise 11
Spine Curls – Exercise 12
Hip Rolls – Exercise 13

Standing at Ease – Exercise 1
The Corkscrew – Exercise 14
Side Reaches – Exercise 16

The Hundred – Exercise 24

The Star – Exercise 27
Rest Position – Exercise 30

Arm Openings – Exercise 39

Day 6
Roll-downs Against the Wall –
  Exercise 2
Relaxation Position – Exercise 4
Breathing Correctly – Exercise 5
Navel to Spine – Exercise 6
Knee Circles & Leg Circles –   Exercise 7
Hamstring Stretch – Exercise 8
Hip Flexors – Exercise 9
Shoulder Drops – Exercise 10
Neck Rolls – Exercise 11
Spine Curls – Exercise 12
Hip Rolls – Exercise 13

Standing at Ease – Exercise 1
Sliding Down the Wall – Exercise 3
Pole Raises – Exercise 18

Single Leg Stretch – Exercise 23

The Cat – Exercise 29
Rest Position – Exercise 30

Arm Openings – Exercise 39

Day 7
Roll-downs Against the Wall –
  Exercise 2
Relaxation Position – Exercise 4
Breathing Correctly – Exercise 5
Navel to Spine – Exercise 6
Knee Circles & Leg Circles – Exercise 7
Hamstring Stretch – Exercise 8
Hip Flexors – Exercise 9
Shoulder Drops – Exercise 10
Nose Spirals – Exercise 11
Spine Curls – Exercise 12
Hip Rolls – Exercise 13

Standing at Ease – Exercise 1
Waist Twist – Exercise 17

Foot Control – Exercises 26A – 26D

The Hundred – Exercise 24

Single Heel-kicks – Exercise 28
Rest Position – Exercise 30

Pillow Squeeze – Exercise 40

THREE SESSIONS A WEEK

Session 1
Roll-downs Against the Wall –
  Exercise 2
Sliding Down the Wall – Exercise 3
Relaxation Position – Exercise 4
Breathing Correctly – Exercise 5
Navel to Spine – Exercise 6
Knee Circles & Leg Circles – Exercise 7
Hamstring Stretch – Exercise 8

Hip Flexors – Exercise 9
Shoulder Drops – Exercise 10
Neck Rolls – Exercise 11
Spine Curls – Exercise 12
Hip Rolls – Exercise 13

Standing at Ease – Exercise 1
The Corkscrew – Exercise 14
Side Reaches – Exercise 16

Curl-ups – Exercise 20
Oblique Curl-ups – Exercise 21
Single Leg Stretch – Exercise 23
Nose Spirals – Exercise 11
Curl-downs – Exercise 25 (if advanced)

The Star – Exercise 27
Rest Position – Exercise 30

The Leg weight series –
  Exercises 31–34

Arm Openings – Exercise 39
Pillow Squeeze – Exercise 40

Session 2

Roll-downs Against the Wall –
  Exercise 2
Relaxation Position – Exercise 4
Breathing Correctly – Exercise 5
Navel to Spine – Exercise 6
Knee Circles & Leg Circles – Exercise 7
Hamstring Stretch – Exercise 8
Hip Flexors – Exercise 9
Shoulder Drops – Exercise 10
Neck Rolls – Exercise 11
Spine Curls – Exercise 12
Hip Rolls – Exercise 13

Standing at Ease – Exercise 1
Waist Twist – Exercise 17
Pole Raises – Exercise 18
Wrists, Hands & Fingers – Exercise 19

Single Leg Stretch – Exercise 23
The Hundred – Exercise 24
Nose Spirals – Exercise 11

Curl-downs –
  Exercise 25 (if advanced)

The Star – Exercise 27
The Cat – Exercise 29
Rest Position – Exercise 30

Foot Control – Exercises 26A – 26D

The Arm weight series –
  Exercises 35 – 38
Arm Openings – Exercise 39
Pillow Squeeze – Exercise 40

Session 3

Roll-downs Against the Wall –
  Exercise 2
Relaxation Position – Exercise 4
Breathing Correctly – Exercise 5
Navel to Spine – Exercise 6
Knee Circles & Leg Circles – Exercise 7
Hamstring Stretch – Exercise 8
Hip Flexors – Exercise 9
Shoulder Drops – Exercise 10
Neck Rolls & Nose Spirals –
  Exercise 11
Spine Curls – Exercise 12
Hip Rolls – Exercise 13

Standing at Ease – Exercise 1
The Corkscrew – Exercise 14
The Samson – Exercise 15

Curl-ups - Exercise 20
Oblique Curl-ups – Exercise 21
Single Leg Stretch – Exercise 23
Curl-downs – Exercise 25 (if advanced)

Single Heel-kicks – Exercise 28
The Cat – Exercise 29
Rest Position & Back-breathing –
  Exercise 30

The Leg weight series –
  Exercises 31 – 34
Arm Openings – Exercise 39
Pillow Squeeze – Exercise 40

TWO SESSIONS A WEEK

Session 1

Roll-downs Against the Wall –
  Exercise 2
Sliding Down the Wall – Exercise 3
Relaxation Position – Exercise 4
Breathing Correctly – Exercise 5
Spine Curls – Exercise 12
Navel to Spine – Exercise 6
Knee Circles & Leg Circles – Exercise 7
Hamstring Stretch – Exercise 8
Hip Flexors – Exercise 9
Shoulder Drops – Exercise 10
Neck Rolls – Exercise 11
Spine Curls – Exercise 12
Hip Rolls – Exercise 13

Standing at Ease – Exercise 1
The Corkscrew – Exercise 14
Side reaches – Exercise 16
Waist Twist – Exercise 17
Wrists, Hands & Fingers – Exercise 19

Curl-ups & Oblique Curl-ups –
  Exercise 20 & 21
Single Leg Stretch – Exercise 23
Nose Spirals – Exercise 11
Curl Downs – Exercise 25

The Star – Exercise 27
Single Heel-kicks – Exercise 28
The Cat – Exercise 29
Rest Position & Back-breathing –
  Exercise 30
Arm and Leg Weights –
  Exercises 35–38

Arm Openings – Exercise 39
Pillow Squeeze – Exercise 40

Session 2

Roll-downs Against the Wall –
  Exercise 2
Sliding Down the Wall – Exercise 3
Relaxation Position – Exercise 4
Breathing Correctly – Exercise 5
Navel to Spine – Exercise 6
Knee Circles & Leg Circles – Exercise 7
Hamstring Stretch – Exercise 8
Hip Flexors – Exercise 9
Shoulder Drops – Exercise 10
Neck Rolls – Exercise 11
Spine Curls – Exercise 12
Hip Rolls – Exercise 13

Standing at Ease – Exercise 1
Pole Raises – Exercise 18
Waist Twist – Exercise 17
The Samson – Exercise15

Curl-ups & Oblique Curl Ups –
  Exercise 20 and 21
Single Leg Stretch – Exercise 23
Nose Spirals – Exercise 11
The Hundred – Exercise 24

The Star – Exercise 27
The Cat – Exercise 29
Rest Position & Back-breathing –
  Exercise 30
Single Heel-kicks – Exercise 28
The Cat – Exercise 29
Rest Position & Back-breathing –
  Exercise 30

Arm & Leg weights – Exercises 35–38
Foot Exercise – Exercise 26

Arm Openings – Exercise 39
Pillow Squeeze – Exercise 40

The Correction of Common Postural Faults

You may be able to recognize yourself as having one of the following common postural problems. This is not particularly easy and it is the kind of advice that you would receive from a trained Pilates teacher. However, you may have been told by your medical practitioner that you have, for example, a hollow or flat back, in which case you will find this chapter helpful.

In reality, most of us are a combination of each type of problem, for example, Kyphosis and Lordosis are often seen together.

We have given you just a few exercises to target each particular problem. This does not mean that they are the only exercises that you should do from the programme, but rather that you should ensure that you include them each time you practise.

Warning: it may be advisable to consult your medical practitioner before starting a remedial programme.

LORDOSIS
This is an overly hollow, arched back.

EXERCISES
2 Roll-downs Against the Wall
3 Sliding Down the Wall
6 Navel to Spine
8 Hamstring Stretch
9 Hip Flexors
13 Hip Rolls
20 Curl-ups
21 Oblique Curl-ups
23 Single Leg Stretch
24 The Hundred
27 The Star
29 The Cat
30 Rest Position
31 Leg weights – Abductor Lifts
40 Pillow Squeeze

KYPHOSIS
This is an exaggerated curve of the thoracic area.

EXERCISES
2 Roll-downs Against the Wall
6 Navel to Spine
10 Shoulder Drops
11 Neck Rolls
14 The Corkscrew
18 Pole Raises
27 The Star
29 The Cat
36 Arm weights – Back-stroke Swimming
39 Arm Openings
Avoid Exercise 35, 'Flys'

THE FLAT BACK

There is little, or no, lumbar curve so that the back appears flat and the pelvis is tilted backwards.

EXERCISES

2 Roll-downs Against the Wall
8 Hamstring Stretch
18 Pole Raises
20 Curl-ups
21 Oblique Curl-ups
23 Single Leg Stretch
27 The Star
28 Single Heel-kicks (The 'sphinx position' is good if you come into it very carefully and it causes you no discomfort. You need not worry about the leg action.)
29 The Cat

THE SWAY BACK

The pelvis has moved forward here, in front of the plumbline, so that the person appears to be swaying backwards. You often see this stance in adolescents, usually temporarily, when they slump into a relaxed pose.

EXERCISES

2 Roll-downs Against the Wall
3 Sliding Down the Wall
8 Hamstring Stretch
9 Hip Flexors (Emphasize the bringing of the knee onto the chest.)
14 The Corkscrew
16 Side Reach in standing position (keep your hips square to the front.)
18 Pole Raises

20 Curl-ups
21 Oblique Curl-ups
23 Single Leg Stretch
40 Pillow Squeeze

A SCOLIOSIS

This is a lateral curve of the spine, which can be in either a 'C' shape or an 'S' shape.

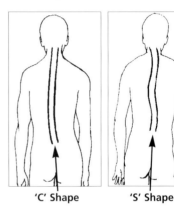

'C' Shape   'S' Shape

By following the overall Body Control programme, lengthening and strengthening the torso, a scoliosis sufferer will benefit greatly. In addition, the sufferer may note that the muscles that require strengthening are those on the outside of the curve. The muscles on the inside of the curve will require stretching.

Further Reading

GENERAL

Dysfunction of Tranversus Abdominis Associated with Chronic Low Back Pain
Article by P.W. Hodges in MPAA Conference Proceedings, 1995.

The Body Has Its Reasons: Anti-Exercises and Self-Awareness
Thérèse Bertherat and Carol Bernstein, Cedar, 1988.

Muscle Control – Pain Control: What Exercises Would You Prescribe?
Article by C.A. Richardson and G.A. Jull in *Manual Therapy*, Pearson Professional Ltd, 1995.

The following books have been invaluable to the authors, both as a source of information and inspiration in the writing of this book:

The Anatomy Coloring Book
Wynn Kapit and Lawrence M. Elson, Harper Collins Publishers, 1977.

The Art of Changing – A New Approach to the Alexander Technique
Glen Park, Ashgrove Press Ltd, 1989.

Back in Action
Sarah Key, Vermilion, 1993.

Back in Ten Minutes
Dr Mary Rintoul and Bernard West, Penguin Books, 1995.

Back Trouble – A New Approach to Prevention and Recovery
Deborah Caplan, Triad Publishing, 1987.

Body Fitness and Exercise – Basic Theory and Practice for Therapists
Mo Rosser, Hodder & Stoughton, 1995.

Body in Action
Sarah Key, Penguin Books/BBC Books, 1992.

Body Stories – A Guide to Experiential Anatomy
Andrea Olsen, Station Hill Press,1991.

Dancing Longer, Dancing Stronger
Andrea Watkins and Priscilla M. Clarkson, Princeton Book Company, 1990.

Human Movement Potential – Its Ideokinetic Facilitation
Lulu Swiegard, Harper & Row Publishers Inc/University Press of America Inc, 1974.

Inside Ballet Technique
Valerie Grieg, Princeton Book Company, 1994.

Manual of Structural Kinesiology
Clem Thompson, Times Mirror/Mosby College Publishing, 1989.

Muscles Testing and Function
Kendall, Kendall and Wadsworth, Williams and Wilkins, Baltimore/London, 1971.

The Muscle Book
Paul Blakey, Bibliotek Books Ltd,1992.

Sports Injuries – Diagnosis and Management for Physiotherapists
Christopher Norris, Butterworth-Heinemann, 1993.

Therapeutic Exercise Foundations and Techniques
Carolyn Kisner and Lynn Allen Colby, F.A. Davis Company, 1990.